SHAW & COPESTAKE

THE COLLECTORS GUIDE TO EARLY SYLVAC
1894-1939

Anthony Van Der Woerd

Georgian Publications P.O. Box 1449, Bath, BA1 3TJ.
in association with
Kingsmead Press.

SHAW & COPESTAKE
THE COLLECTORS GUIDE TO EARLY SYLVAC
1894-1939
Anthony Van Der Woerd

ISBN 1 85026 015 X

Georgian Publications P.O. Box 1449, Bath, BA1 3TJ.
in association with Kingsmead Press.

Design And Production By:
Corinth Publication Services Backwell Avon

CONTENTS

		Page
Acknowledgements		4
How to use this Book		5
Introduction		7
1.	A Brief History of the Shaw & Copestake Factory	9
2.	Backstamping with Factory Marks	17
3.	Decorating Techniques	23
4.	How to date Shaw & Copestake	27
5.	The Products of the Shaw & Copestake Factory-I	29
	Vases	29
	Illustrations	32 – 43
	Wash Sets, Chamber Pots and Dressing Table Sets	29
	Illustrations	44 – 48
	Clocks and Clock Sets	29
	Clock Movements – By Michael Turner	30 – 31
	Illustrations	49 –56
	Plates, Centrepieces and Jardinieres	31
	Illustrations	57 – 59
	Jugs and Cheese Dishes	31
	Illustrations	60 – 62
6.	The Products of the Shaw & Copestake Factory-II	63
	Cellulose Hollow Ware	63
	Illustrations	64 – 68
	Cellulose Figures, Animals and Novelties	63
	Illustrations	69 – 75
	Art Deco Style Ware	63 – 64
	Illustrations	76 – 80
7.	Registered Designs Numbers	81 – 116
8.	Shape Guide	117 – 138
9.	Mould Number List and Dates	139 – 153
10.	Decoration Numbers and Dates with Historical Notes	155 – 158

ACKNOWLEDGEMENTS

Many people and organisations have helped me in the course of this project. I would like to thank them all, especially the following :

Nick Rees M. A. and Leslie Howe F.D.S. whose invaluable support and advice made this book possible. They have provided very many magnificent pieces from their collection, helped with the photography and made helpful suggestions about layout etc. Above all they have given unstintingly of their advice and friendship.

Mick and Derry Collins of the SylvaC Collector's Club who supplied missing factory documents and supplied much needed information.

Susan Verbeek, the author of The SylvaC Story and The SylvaC Companion, first for the impetus which her books have provided and also for supplying both information and contacts.

Malcolm Harris for his keen research.

Darrell Willis-Utting for his unbounded enthusiasm.

The following have kindly lent items which have been photographed and/or illustrated :
Pat and Alex Howe, George and Olive Caple, Darrell Willis-Utting, Mrs Dickinson, Ken Dore, Francis and Violet Brown, Malcolm Harris, Susan Verbeek, Mick and Derry Collins, Brian Staley, Mr & Mrs C. Barber, and Mr & Mrs Stiles (Australia).

I have been greatly assisted by Mrs Kathleen Hippisley and Neil McKay with my research into the historical background; while the Hanley Library, the Stoke-On-Trent City Museum and Art Gallery also proved very helpful. The Public Record Office at Kew has been most obliging and guided me through their labyrinthine shelves and also provided photographs of early materials.

PHOTOGRAPHS

The photography was undertaken by Leslie Howe, Nick Rees and myself under the supervision of the well known West of England photographer Roland Prosser. Other photographs have been acknowledged where they appear in the text.

IMPORTANT NOTICE

HOW TO USE THIS BOOK

No description, however accurate, can hope to convey the subtle charm of Shaw & Copestake, and so to avoid the need for lengthy descriptions, every effort has been made to illustrate the maximum possible number of Shaw & Copestake major shapes and patterns by full colour photographs.

A date for each mould or pot is calculated by reference to the impressed numbers on the base of the article in question: this may well pre-date the decoration.

Each illustration shows the mould number of individual pieces together with the pattern name and number if this is known. More detailed descriptions, measurements and dates are given in the list of mould numbers in Chapter 9 page 139 which should be used in conjunction with Chapter 8 page 117 on shapes.

Many of the earlier vases etc. are more accurately dated by their decorations, a list of which may be found in Chapter 10.

Decorations lasted a variable length of time and some of the more popular continued for very many years after they were first introduced. This has made it almost impossible to give specific dates for decorations and I have concentrated on the year in which the design in question was introduced.

Unless otherwise stated, all illustrated items are marked with a "Daisy" or mould number, or both.

Cellulose and matt ware were not generally "Daisy" marked: see Chapter 2 on Factory Marks.

Illustrations are sometimes accompanied by the following abbreviations.

NN ... No number

Des No ... Design/Decoration number

INTRODUCTION

The Shaw & Copestake Company was part of the long tradition of pottery manufacturing in Staffordshire. Situated at Longton, one of the six towns which together make up the Potteries, the Company was part of a pottery-making tradition stretching back to pre-historic times, no doubt taking advantage of the nearby abundance of coal and clay. Despite the Industrial Revolution, mechanisation in the traditional pottery factory occurred very gradually and when the factory was founded in the 1890's most processes were still executed by hand or with the aid of some rudimentary mechanical devices. Output continued at a leisurely pace until well after the Second World War when mass production techniques were eventually introduced; it was not until the new SylvaC factory opened in 1955 that the production was completely mechanised.

The aim of the Shaw & Copestake Company, in common with most other 19th Century pottery manufacturers, was to exploit the newly invented "white earthenware", turning out products which were both cheap and durable. They came in all shapes, sizes and colours. As well as saturating the home market the new wares were shipped abroad in prodigious quantities, usually to the Commonwealth and Colonies and also to South America.

The early factory records are sparse but the products themselves, while conforming to the prevailing trends of pottery manufacturers generally, depict a unique style which is recognisable to this day.

This book attempts to show the output of the factory from its beginnings in 1894 when the high glaze and heavy gilding of the late Victorian era was supreme, moving on to the figurines and cellulose finished products of the 1920's. It finishes with the Art Deco creations of the 1930's including the new "mattglaze" which made its appearance a few years before the Second World War.

Like many obsessions my own collection started by chance. At a dinner party in the late 1980's a stylish SylvaC jug was produced and further investigation suggested that here was the ideal combination of artistic distinctiveness at a reasonable price. I set about collecting in earnest the next day with a visit to a local market where a vase with the characteristic daisy mark was on offer. I snapped it up not quite believing that it was from the same factory as the SylvaC I had just been shown. Its style and appearance was so different. The mystery was solved after a hurried consultation in the reference section at a local book shop : what I had bought was one of the early outputs of the factory later specialising in SylvaC ware - Shaw & Copestake. As I added more and more pieces to my collection the attractions of these astonishingly original pieces grew stronger and I realised that this is what I wanted to collect.

It soon became clear, however, that no early records or catalogues existed and that there was an obvious need for an illustrated guide to the production of the early factory. It was then I decided to write this book.

Because of the dearth of published material it was necessary to go straight to the sources and so I have spent many hours at the Public Record Office and at museums drawing together the scant references to Shaw & Copestake. Like other researchers I have been a frequent visitor to the Hanley Library and my journeys there, though long, have always been rewarded. Finally the publishing of Susan Verbeek's book added momentum to my labours.

The book's aim is to provide a practical work of reference to to assist in the identification of patterns and shapes, but at the same time to kindle an interest in the astonishing range and variety of this most remarkable factory. It may not be possible to slip it into your pocket or handbag when you go round the fairs but your collecting will be more informed and rewarding if you have it close at hand when you find your next piece of Shaw & Copestake.

CHAPTER 1

A BRIEF HISTORY OF THE SHAW & COPESTAKE FACTORY

It was a chance discovery by George and Olive Caple of an original half-tone printing plate belonging to Sheaf Art Pottery nestling among some old Shaw & Copestake advertising blocks that first put me onto the scent of the origins of the Shaw & Copestake Factory. After searching through records at the Hanley Library and consulting Malcolm Chapman, a former Director, and other experts it became clear that the first factory was set up by William Shaw under the name Sheaf Pottery at Normacot Road, Longton, in 1894. (Normacot Road was originally called Wheat Sheaf Street).

It has not been possible to pinpoint the exact location of the original factory. It is possible that the original site was in Sheaf Passage which ran alongside the later factory between Normacot Road and Webberly Lane. A pottery works operating from this site is mentioned in an early mortgage deed.

Sheaf Pottery Advert Pottery Gazette, 1st June 1895.

It is commonly thought that the Company was founded by William Shaw in 1894 and operated from the Sheaf Pottery site.

Sometime between January and April 1896 Sheaf Pottery moved to Commerce Street, Longton. Such moves were fairly routine at the turn of the century, with a new factory needing little more than a kiln and some basic premises, with no necessity to conform to planning or other regulations.

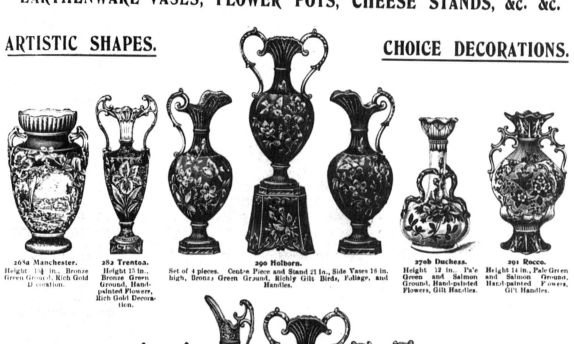

Shaw & Copestake Advert Pottery Gazette March 1904, Same vases are shown in the Sheaf Art Pottery illustration.

*William Shaw Advert
Pottery Gazette
February 1901.*

In about 1902 or 1903 Mr Shaw took on his first partner, Mr Copestake. Very little is known about him, not even his Christian name. It seems he settled into the Sylvan Works, Longton around 1902-1903. The partnership was very brief indeed because by November 1903 Mr Copestake had departed the scene and his place was taken by Richard Hull Senior who had recently returned from Canada. It is thought that Mr Hull bought out Mr Copestake's share and although he no longer had any dealings with the factory the partnership still bore his name, which is, incidently, a fairly common Staffordshire surname.

The Company's own publication *Shaw & Copestake's History in Brief* published for their customers, gives a different, and, I believe, inaccurate account of these early years. It suggests that a Mr Hull Senior was taken into partnership in 1900, although this is contradicted in Mr Shaw's own obituary where the date of 1898 is given.

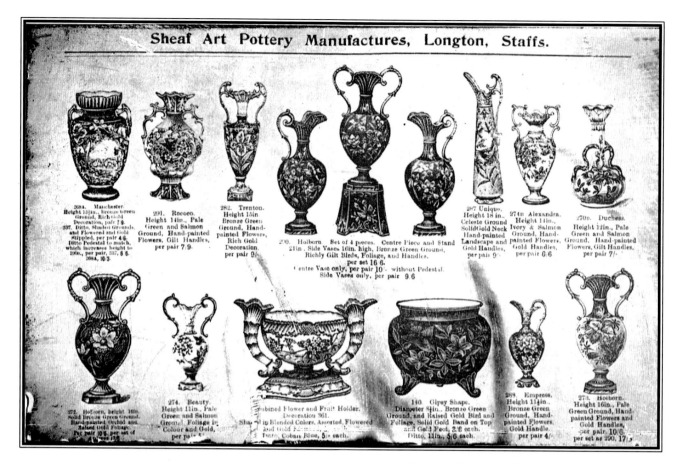

Sheaf pottery Catalogue picture showing
Holborn vase and others circa 1901

In fact the partnership deed between William Shaw of 340 Uttoxeter Road, Longton and Richard Hull of Voryn, Trentham Road, Longton is dated 3rd November 1903, which suggests that until that date Mr Shaw was operating either as a sole proprietor, or in partnership with someone else, i.e. Mr Copestake.

This view of early events is confirmed by two advertisements appearing in the Pottery Gazette in the early months of 1901. William Shaw is now seen to be operating from King Street, another address in Longton, as a sole proprietor. The advertisement in the February edition was enhanced by an illustration of the Holborn vase which was obviously taken from the Sheaf Pottery Catalogue published at about that time.

The early years were devoted to expansion. Numerous agencies were set up in the Colonies, some as early as 1903.

The years immediately preceding the First World War continued to be healthy in terms of trade and by 1917 further loans were taken out with the ever obliging Garle family.

The personal representatives of William Garle who had been helpful to the partnership in 1906, again proved a useful source of capital.

Although there was a skeleton work force during the First World War, production picked up by the early 1920's, and perhaps the most important event in this decade was the arrival of Richard Hull Jnr in 1924, aged 18. In later years he very much prided himself on having worked his way up from the factory floor. This appears not to have taken long because by 1929 his influence on new products was considerable. In those days most potteries had no such thing as a design department or an in-house product manager but relied on the ingenuity of owners or ordinary members of staff to dream up new ideas. By the late 1920's it was becoming obvious that the original wares had had their day and Richard Hull, who had a keen commercial eye, began to look round for other wares to introduce such as figures and novelty items.

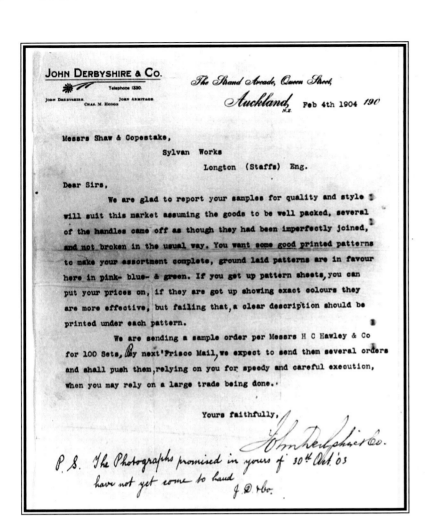

Agencies were set up in New Zealand, Australia, Canada and the West Indies

Illustration deed showing amount and property including Sheaf Pottery. By 1906 £1900 was borrowed on mortgage.

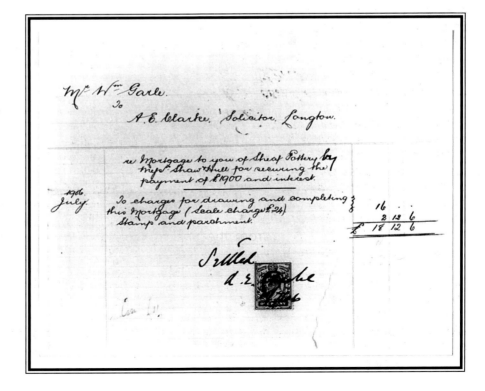

Malcolm Chapman tells an interesting story of how Richard Hull Jnr travelled abroad collecting new ideas and products which he purchased with his own money and brought back to William Shaw who would sometimes thoroughly disapprove. The Bunnies, for example, believed to have been spotted by young Mr Hull in France, turned out to be a runaway success as far afield as New Zealand. They were commended in a letter from the factory to the agent in Auckland in the following terms

Rabbits & Dogs etc.

"We find these novelty lines are very good sellers in the Departmental Stores, especially the Rabbits of which we have sold several hundreds of dozens, one Firm placing an order for 12,200"

1917 Indenture

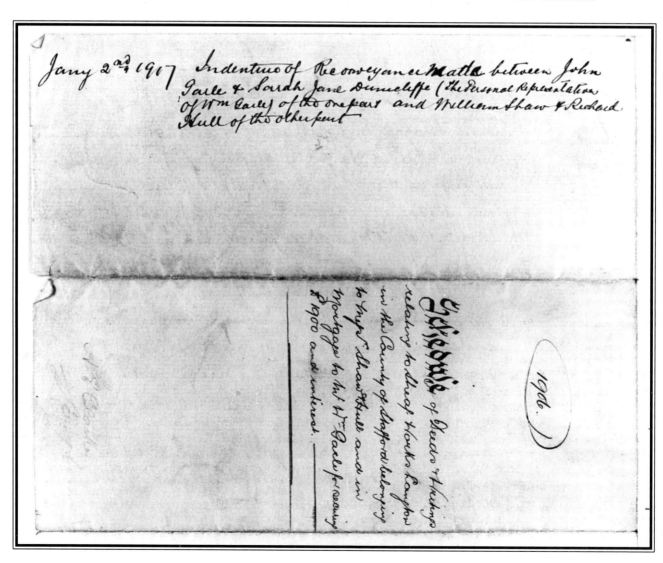

Barclays Bank Limited.

Longton, STAFFORDSHIRE.

ALL LETTERS
TO BE ADDRESSED TO
THE MANAGER.

FWT/ESH
TELEPHONE
LONGTON 3518.

21st November, 19 29

Messrs. Shaw & Copestake,
   Sylvan Works,
     LONGTON,
      Staffs.

Dear Sirs,

     Scottish Union and National Fire Policies.

     We enclose an endorsement slip for attaching to Fire Policy No. 4/5707317 which relates to your using Cellulose Lacquer.

     We have also received an endorsement slip for Policy No. 4/5707336 and as this Policy is in our possession, we have attached the slip thereto.

     The endorsement reads:-

"8th November, 1929, It has been intimated that a quantity of cellulose lacquer, not exceeding 35 gallons is stored on the gound floor of the building within described, in drums each of five gallons capacity. Premium and all other Conditions unaltered."

                     Yours faithfully,

                           MANAGER.

*Illustration
Barclays Bank –
Note the use of
cellulose lacquer*

The late 1920's and early 1930's, despite the Depression, saw further increases in production as can be seen from the letter sent to the factory by their bankers, Barclays, in Longton. The Bank, ever prudent, was keen to ensure that its investment was properly insured.

Shaw & Copestake were incorporated as a limited company in 1936. In 1938 they merged with Thomas Lawrence Limited (Falcon Ware). The merger was, no doubt, very good for business but very confusing for the collector because of the decision to discontinue early Shaw & Copestake numbers and instead use Falcon Ware numbers which had not then been utilised.

The history ends in 1982 when the company went into voluntary liquidation. All the company records including pattern books, and other materials, which made up the life blood of the factory were dumped on a skip and destroyed.

Particulars of Insurance Claim 1930's

570735S

PARTICULARS OF CLAIM

To be given in detail, and suitable allowances made for depreciation by wear and tear.

Description of Property Destroyed or damaged.	Date of Purchase	COST PRICE			Actual value at date of fire.			Amount claimed after allowance for value of salvage.		
26 Crates	1929/30.	10	8	-	9	2	-	9	2	-
One extending three storey ladder	1922	6	3	-	4	-	-	4	-	-
3 Placers Oven Horses	-	2	5	-	1	15	-			
3 Casting troughs.										
1 Gab. Dust Exhausting Hood.										
3 tons. 10 cwts. Oat Straw	May & June 1930	11	17	6	11	17	6	11	17	6
½ Bag Linen Dusters		1	12	6	1	12	6	1	12	6
½ Bag Engine Waste			17	-		17	-		17	-
4 Padlocks	1929		10	6		7	9		7	9
15 cwts.Woodwool	May & June 1930	6	-	-	6	-	-	6	-	-
12 Doz.Chambers White	May & June 1930	8	2	-	8	2	-	4	1	-
12 " Chambers Deco. & Gilt	do.	10	4	-	10	4	-	5	2	-
12 Doz.Vases 538 asst.	do.	6	-	-	6	-	-	3	-	-
3 Clock sets 651/2.										
6 " " 608/9										
30 " " 605/6										
12 " " 695/037										
Moulds.								50	-	-
								96	19	9

CHAPTER 2

BACK STAMPING WITH FACTORY MARKS

Factory markings, although quite methodical, were sometimes a little haphazard. Thus not every item was stamped, this being particularly so in groups or sets where only a single item would be identified. Mould numbers and "Daisy" marks combined with the "Made in England" are quite distinctive as is the lettering on certain items, although any one or indeed all of these markings could be left off.

According to Goddens Encyclopaedia of British Pottery and Porcelain Marks the "Daisy" mark started around 1925. The impetus for this seems to be an Act of Parliament requiring goods to be stamped with the words "Made in England" if produced after 1920. The English statute followed an earlier United States Enactment of 1891 requiring articles for import into the U.S.A. to have the country of origin stamped on them, so that goods made in Staffordshire would be stamped "England" while those manufactured in Liege would be stamped "France." There is some evidence to suggest that in the case of Shaw & Copestake the "Daisy" mark (which of course includes "Made in England" within its circumference) was used much earlier than the 1920's. Mrs Violet Brown who knew Mr Shaw and family well recalls her father receiving a hamper of crockery, each stamped with the "Daisy" mark as a reward for finding Mr Shaw's dog.

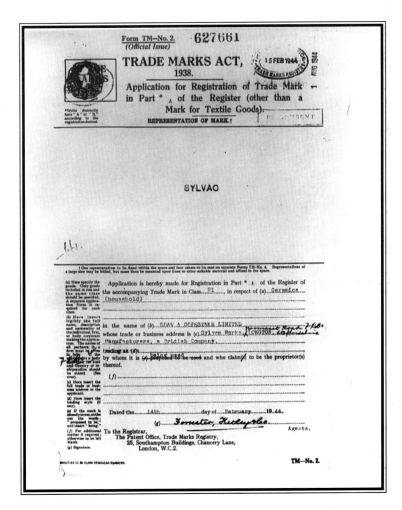

SylvaC copy Certificate application. The trade name was renewed on the 15th February 1951 and subsequently on the 15th February 1979 which will remain in force until 15th February 1993

She vividly remembers that this happened the year before the family moved from their Post Office in 1913. If, therefore, her memory is accurate, and she is a most precise lady, it seems to follow that the "Daisy" was in use by 1912 and perhaps for some years earlier. It may be that Mr Shaw, who like many Victorians and Edwardians of his day was very patriotic, which he combined with an evident keenness to export (as can be seen from his letters of 1903) began to stamp his wares with their country of origin from the early 1900's.

The Pottery Gazette Directory which is normally a good source of information is of little help in establishing the date of the origin of the "Daisy" mark and only establishes that it was in use in 1929. A decade later, in 1939, the Gazette shows both the normal "Daisy" mark and the new "Combined Daisy" mark with the word "SylvaC" and "Semi-porcelain" incorporated within it, in current use. Goddens also refers to the "Combined Daisy" mark and states that the mark has been used between 1936-40. This is probably correct, but in my view it could have been used one or two years earlier.

"Scello" was the first name adopted by Shaw & Copestake for their cellulose products before the name "SylvaC" was used. No doubt it appealed to Mr Shaw and Mr Hull because of the use of the factory initials SC as the opening letters of the word. A similar idea was adopted again in 1935 with the invention of the more familiar SylvaC name.

It is said that Richard Hull thought up the name SylvaC by using the works name Sylvan and changing the N to a C which stood for Copestake. This seems highly plausible and appears to have occurred late in 1935 or in 1936. It was not used consistently on wares until much later. The name "SylvaC" was not registered until 15th February 1944, by Certificate No. 627661.

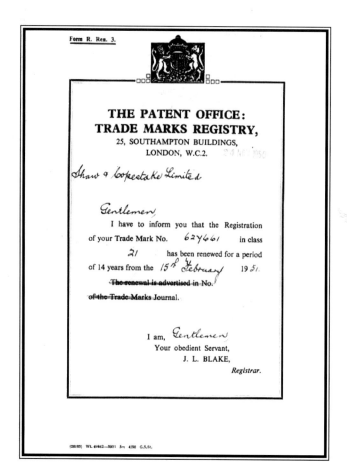

SylvaC renewal certificate

The "Daisy" marks were used until the end of the 1930's. Gradually, as the patterns and wares changed, the "Daisy" was replaced by the name "SylvaC" which began to be impressed next to the mould numbers on the base of the newer novelties. Sometimes sticky "SylvaC" labels were also used when there was no other identification. Unfortunately these have a tendency to wash off. The "Daisy" mark was not used after the Second World War.

early), black (standard), and gold (used probably on prestige wares or those with considerable gold decoration).

It is rare to find the combined marks used on early cellulose, but it is seen with the "Semi-Porcelain" deleted.

THE DAISY MARK

The standard mark is an eight petalled daisy and dots, with "Made in England" inside the circumference and a small daisy in the centre. The daisy occurs in three colours, green (possibly

Standard Daisy c. 1912 – 39

Small Daisy only 1912 – 39

Daisy with SylvaC and semi-porcelain known as the combined mark c. 1935 –39

Daisy with SylvaC only c.1935 – 37

IMPRESSED MARKS

Numbers, names, and "Made in England" are also found on the base of many wares. The mould numbers started around 1906 and a full list of numbers are given on pages 139 – 153

Applied Registered design number and mould number 1913

Made in England with mould number c. 1928 onward.

Silvo early 1930's – 1939

Napier mid 1920's – 1939

Roman c.1928 – 36

Portland vase 1927 – 1936

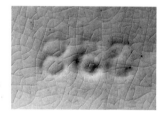

Anomalies 338 mirrored numbers any date

SylvaC late 1930 onward

Portland vase 1927 – 1936

LABELS *applied or painted*

"Scello" Ware early name
for cellulose products c.
1928 – 1935

Wild Duck c. 1931
onwards

Harvest Poppy c.1932 –
1939 (Carnation not
illustrated – 1934 – 1936)

Cornflower c.1936 – 1939

Egyptian c.1932 – 1936

SylvaC labels silver and
black c. 1935/6 – c. 1940

SylvaC label black and
white late 1930's – 1940's
plus

Other Marks

Hand Painted 1920's and
1930's

Moonlight 1500 c.1920's

Base showing decoration
number from c.1919
onwards

CHAPTER 3

DECORATING TECHNIQUES

The Development of Decoration in the Pottery Trade

With Mintons and Wedgwood in the vanguard, the pottery trade during the latter half of the 19th century began to produce a large variety of colourful new glazes and styles. The prize for innovation in this respect must be awarded to Mintons who opened an Art Studio in Kensington Gore in 1870, having the enterprising object of employing students from nearby Art Schools to produce pieces which were both hand made and hand painted. These products very quickly came to be known as "Art Pottery".

This term was quickly appropriated by other manufacturers to describe their own wares, even though these were very often mass produced. Thus although Mr Shaw's Sheaf Art Pottery was hand decorated, the wares themselves were produced in factory moulds and were not hand turned; no doubt the absence of a Trades Description Act assisted in this enhancing of the products.

Following the widespread success of Art Pottery, manufacturing styles progressed to Art Nouveau which was introduced around 1893. In its early days Art Nouveau was, of course, very avant-garde and most often found in the salons of sophisticated metropolitan life. The more conservative potteries largely ignored the new fashion during its pioneering days but by the 1920's when it was firmly rooted in popular taste it was taken up by many of the manufacturers including Shaw & Copestake. –See vase illustration number page 80.

Apart from hand finishing, another form of decoration was by means of transfers printed from copper plate engravings. This enjoyed immense popularity from the mid 19th century with the first attempts at lithography in Staffordshire being made as early as 1840. This was a very embryonic affair and lithographic transfers were not produced on a commercial scale until 1895 when Pierre Rataud set up his Potters Decorative Supply Company at Hanley.

The Decorative Techniques Used By Shaw & Copestake

Shaw & Copestake used all the basic techniques currently available to fulfil its constant aim of producing wares in quantity which both looked good and were sold at a price ordinary people could afford.

An early technique was to put on the "background" (ground) colour by dipping or spraying (aerographing) one, two, or three colour coats which were often shaded to create highlights as a background. The items were then largely hand painted and gilded. During these early days there were many completely hand painted designs of flowers, figures in national costume, landscapes etc.

By the early 1900's the factory was making full use of the improved decorative techniques of the industry by using coloured transfer tissues with hand embellishments. Sometimes the results were uneven and one can often see the creases and joins of the early transfers where the decorators struggled to place them on curved surfaces. It was not until the invention of Duplex paper in 1935, which permitted transfers to be used on curved surfaces, that the process of lithographic transfer was able to solve the problem of decorating rounded products.

Shaw & Copestake were one of the earliest users of this process and were persevering with lithographic transfer patters even before the task was made easier with the new invention. In 1934 letters offered lithographic transfer patterns to customers abroad.

Some of the transfers used by the factory were employed by them exclusively, either because of rights acquired in a registered design or following some agreement with the transfer manufacturer, while others were used in common with rival factories.

Shaw & Copestake, in fact, only had the exclusive use of two registered designs, both owned by Davis & Company: Lovebirds and Venetian (see Registered Designs –pages 87 – 88). The registration of a design did not, of course, permit exclusive use in perpetuity. Unless the registration was renewed after the initial five years for a further five year period then anyone was at liberty to make use of it. Both "Lovebirds" and "Venetian" were allowed to lapse after the initial registration period but this may have been a mistake in the case of "Lovebirds" because parts of the design were subsequently used by other manufacturers. The method most commonly used by Shaw & Copestake to put out exclusive designs, however, was by a private agreement with the design owners: thus Moonlight, Inns of England, and Scenes of the Old Country were all exclusive to Shaw & Copestake although none of these were registered.

The remainder of the factory's output related to non-exclusive designs which they shared with other manufacturers. For this reason it is hazardous to seek to authenticate a piece by reference to its design alone. This can only be undertaken with safety for those designs which are known to be exclusive to Shaw & Copestake. Such designs are appropriately marked in the list of decorations on – page 155.

Some transfers were very popular indeed and were used in varying combinations and in different sequences, often producing new patterns from the resulting configurations. It is worthwhile memorising some of the more common ones since they are a good indicator of authenticity. It is sometimes difficult to spot a quite common transfer because they were often used upside down, particularly as part of the decoration of pairs. Take care before rejecting, for example, a pair of vases on the ground that the decorations are not precisely symmetrical. Very often the transfers used to decorate one of a pair would be placed upside down deliberately.

Lustreware

This is created by applying a thin metallic coating in liquid form to the surface of a glaze which is subsequently fired at a higher temperature than normal to give an iridescent glazed finish. A good example is to be found in illustration PL20 on page   – 44. Pink lustre was also made.

Cellulose

From the late 1920's the factory began to produce a large range of items in cellulose finish. This is a paint finish which was varnished for protection. This was an inexpensive method of producing a wide range of colourful items. Because of its importance this will be dealt with in greater detail in chapter 6 page 63. See also under Scello Ware –page 18 & 21.

Blue/Black Wares With Relief Decoration

Cellulose was also used in the late 1920's and 1930's to produce the factory's imitation of Wedgwood's celebrated Jasper ware. The figures and motifs were applied beforehand in slip and then fired. The item to be decorated was then dipped in blue or black paint. When dry the applied decorations were painted in white by hand. The effect is very imitative of Wedgwood, at least from a distance.

Shaw & Copestake occasionally marked these cellulose items
"Scello" Ware see pages18 & 21 of Chapter 2
Backstamping with Factory Marks –illustration page 56.

Matt Glaze

Around the mid 1930's Richard Hull Jnr collaborated with a firm of paint and glaze manfuacturers, Harrison & Son of Hanley, to perfect the matt glaze which has become the hallmark of SylvaC for today's collector. The initial output was in plain colours of green, (very popular in the 1930's), dark blue, brown, and beige although other colours were added later. The dark blue and brown colours had lower production runs and, as a consequence, are rarer. llustration page 77

Condition and Restoration

Many products are passed over by collectors as not worth acquiring because of perceived "faults" in their appearance. This is often a mistake. It should be remembered that the factory never aimed to produce products of exquisite quality; their enduring charm is to be found in their primitive elegance and is akin to the attraction of a naive painting or a homely Staffordshire figure. Thus the presence of imperfections in the decoration or on the glaze are unimportant. Small imperfections were often painted over by the factory and should not be considered a fault. Similar considerations apply to the glaze which often gives the appearance of a series of fine cracks completely covering its surface. Known as "crazing" this happened in the factory as the result of the firing process and is more a sign of authenticity than a fault.

Restoration is always a controversial subject; some experienced collectors eschew all attempts while others take a more liberal view. Provided the product is sold as "a restored" item with a corresponding reduction in the purchase price it can still form a worthwhile addition to a collection. New materials and techniques make repairs increasingly difficult to detect and provided the work is well done an otherwise blemished article can be restored to something approaching its former glory.

Bread Plate, showing crazing

Registered Design Number 634174 – see page 85

CHAPTER 4

HOW TO DATE SHAW & COPESTAKE

The dating of the factory's products has been extremely difficult. The dates of registered designs, when found in conjunction with a mould number, have been used to date the introduction of the design; although it is anyone's guess how long a particular pattern or shape remained in production.

There are two distinct methods of dating Shaw & Copestake wares

I: Since all mould numbers were used in sequence their presence on almost all the bases of each of the wares can be used to date when a design was first introduced. This is done by reference to the date of the Registered Design kept in the Public Record Office (where applicable) and calculating accordingly.

The sequential mould number method broke down in 1938 with the merger with the Thomas Lawrence Factory when a large number of the "older designs" were discontinued and their numbers re-used in the Falconware Factory for the new product. The re-used numbers largely followed Falconware's own system and were embossed, rather than impressed although this was not always the case.

A list of mould numbers with dates can be found on page 139 which also (where appropriate) briefly describes the popular design influences. I have used these as a guide to further pinpoint the date of the ware in question. Since Shaw & Copestake were manufacturing for the popular market their developing shapes and mouldings are a good guide to the popular taste. This is strikingly evident in the Art Deco Period.

But even this method has its pitfalls because as with other factories (for instance Royal Worcester) older products were resurrected at a later date and then given a different decoration.

II: By reference to the decoration or glaze. This tends to be more accurate and a list of patterns with their dates, numbers and descriptions are set out on page 155. Historical notes and dates are also given where appropriate.

Vase 611

CHAPTER 5

THE PRODUCTS OF THE SHAW & COPESTAKE FACTORY – 1

VASES

This ubiquitous adornment of every British home from country manorhouse to workman's cottage was used more for decoration than utility. Vases were sold largely in pairs although larger three, four and even five piece sets were manufactured. Collectors should bear in mind that there will almost always be slight variations in the size of a pair or in the larger sets because of differentials in the shrinkage rate when fired. Collectors should not be put off if one member of a set is slightly taller or broader. Another pitfall stems from the differences in decoration. It is quite wrong to assume that each part of a set must be identical in decoration. Very often transfers were simply used upside down. This does not mean that a mistake has been made or that two disparate items have been wrongly married up.

See Illustrations on pages 32 – 43.

WASH SETS, CHAMBER POTS & DRESSING TABLE SETS

It now seems hard to believe that not so long ago wash sets were an essential part of bedroom furniture. Before the days of running hot water they were used as much for hygiene as decoration. Their potential as an example of the paintresses' art was soon recognised by the factory girls who used their large surfaces to show off their painting skills. Wash stand sets complete with matching jugs, sometimes known as "ewers", bowls, soap dishes, tooth brush holders and chamber pots were extravagantly decorated in a myriad of eye catching patterns. For the most part the shapes used were Napier and Silvo. A shape guide is to be found on page 117

Illustrations pages 44 – 48

CLOCKS & CLOCK SETS

These were one of the most important products of the factory by the 1920's and 1930's and as far as I can tell Shaw & Copestake were among the largest producers of clocks and clock sets.

The origins of the clock set go back to the 18th and 19th centuries when the grand houses of the nobility had their mantlepieces adorned with fine clocks and also with pairs of vases which were often imported. Although placed alongside the clock the vases were not made as part of a three piece set; they complemented rather than matched the timepiece. These fine examples of the period were plainly beyond the means of ordinary people, but the emerging middle classes were eager to emulate the aristocracy. They too were keen to enhance their mantlepieces and so matching clock sets were manufactured for this purpose.

Although most clocks were made to accompany specific vases the Company was not above putting together a different combination to satisfy a customer.

By far the most common finishes are those in standard gloss glaze and cellulose although rare examples of parts of sets in matt green and a set in a rather unstable paint finish do exist.

Illustration pages 49 – 56. Where clocks are shown without their accompanying vases their reference numbers are given.

THE CLOCK MOVEMENTS - by Michael Turner, Sotheby's Clocks and Watch Department.

The clocks made by Shaw & Copestake were invariably fitted with German mass produced movements usually designed to fit a 2 $\frac{1}{4}$" aperture, although larger sizes have been noted. These simple little movements have stood the test of time remarkably well, and the original manufacturers would have been amazed to know that their modest products are still functioning more than 50 years after manufacture.

The actual movement comprises a pair of circular skeletonised brass plates held together by hexagonal nuts and containing an open mainspring driving a set of brass wheels and lantern pinions leading to the escapement, of regulating mechanism, which is of the pinpallet and balance wheel type.

A typical clock movement

This form of escapement has been used in alarm clocks and cheaper mantle clocks since the last quarter of the 19th century; it is easy to produce and reliable over a long period. The dials are either cardboard or silvered metal and the whole movement is most usually contained in a pin sleeve (concealed by the case) with a polished brass or chrome bezel and back. Many of the mechanisms examined have been drilled to accept an alarm train although none of the movements in Shaw & Copestake cases seem to have been fitted with an alarm. The manufacturers obviously supplied the movements, with or without alarm, to various wholesalers who fitted them to a variety of cases. I cannot stress too strongly the importance of preserving and restoring these original clock movements whenever possible. Although similar movements are still made today making it all too easy to buy a modern movement and fit it to an old case, in my view this practice is little short of vandalism if it results in an old movement being discarded. The value of the complete clock is degraded and from the aesthetic point of view the modern movements usually have over-fancy French style dials which are quite inappropriate when fitted to a Shaw & Copestake case. Even those modern movements that have plainer dials are not satisfactory as the style of the dial and the hands on the examples I have examined have never been exact reproductions of the original. Wherever possible restoration of the original should be attempted; many clock makers will tend to dismiss this type of movement and state that it is "not worth" repairing. There are, however, more enlightened horologists who will appreciate the importance of preserving an original movement when it is an integral part of a highly collectable item.

One of the most frequently encountered problems is discolouration of the dial caused, most often, by too liberal an application of oil to a non-functioning movement. It is possible to remove a certain amount of staining with detergent or bleach but if the problem is serious a replacement dial should be found and sometimes the most satisfactory solution is to fit a photographic reproduction of a good original dial. If this appears too daunting it may be helpful to look through the classified advertisements in one of the monthly horological magazines where a number of dial restorers advertise their trade. In this regard I am happy to recommend Meadows & Passmore, Medmaw House, Farningham Road, Crowborough, East Sussex, TN6 2JP; telephone 0892 662255; Fax 0892 662277.

PLATES, CENTRE PIECES, JARDINIERES

Centre pieces and rose bowls were often presentation pieces and were made in conjunction with a large range of jardinieres. The variety is enormous, spanning from the first years of production with extravagant gilt designs to the later stylized tree trunks complete with hopping bunnies which are so memorable a feature of SylvaC in post-war years.

See illustrations pages 57 – 59.

JUGS AND CHEESE DISHES

In the days before milk bottles and modern packaging jugs played an important part in household life. They were in constant use not only for storing and pouring milk, but also for use in connection with sauces, custards, jellies, not forgetting home brewed beer and cider. Although forming part of the workaday equipment they often did duty as part of a fine display on the kitchen dresser. Many of the best examples seem too good for every day use and were made primarily with decoration in mind or at least were only used "for best". Jugs are most often found in sets of three but Shaw & Copestake did manufacture four and five set pieces in some shapes – see illustration page 60 – 62.

SHAW & COPESTAKE, LONGTON.

4 piece Holborn set from the Pottery Gazette 1904

NN   *NN*

1. *Pair of side vases. NN.*
   Height 16in. Hand painted.

2. *The Holborn vase. Height*
   16in.NN. Hand painted
   on bronze green ground.

NN

The above two illustrations show the Holborn set
similar to the 1904 advertisements.

354

3. *Holborn vase and stand. Height 21in. Pink rose transfer. Mould number 354 impressed in base. No daisy mark. Post 1904 model, slightly altered with shorter neck flutings and embossed leaves below. The fan shape mouth of the vase is slightly different. Circa 1914.*

NN

4. *The Manchester vase from
the original 1904 range. NN.*

565

6a. *565 Des No 2431,*

5. *Portland Vase 11$\frac{1}{2}$ h 8$\frac{1}{2}$ dia.
Impressed 'PORTLAND VASE'
on base. Des No 2334. (Also
seen in blue cellulose finish
–see page 138).*

NN

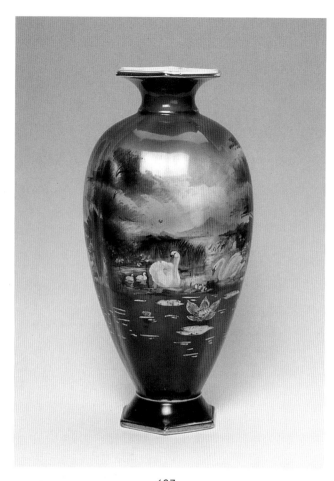

627

6C. *627 Des No 2495,*

279

6b. *279 Swans, Vase Reg No 626318 date 1913 see page 82*

6d. *562 Roses.*

562

419   446   422

7. Des.No2007. Lovebirds Reg
     No 716616 1925. Page 87

8. Left: Venetian
     Des No 1977,
     Centre;
     Lovebirds Des
     No 2007, Right;
     Venetian Des no
     1977. Both
     patterns are
     Reg No 716616
     1925.
     Pages 87 & 88

281   496   629   387

582

420

449

9. 'Moonlight' Des No 1500.

10. 'Moonlight'
Des No 1500.

510

75

445

375   376   375

11. 'Moonlight' Des No 1500.

12. Pink Roses on black.

416   357   416

445   548

13. 445 Basket of Fruit Des No 1996,
548 'Moonlight' 1500'.

14. Cascading English Roses.

371   562   587

255

338

365

15. Rural Scenes. Vases 255 and
365 are similar to the Holborn
shape. No 365 signed
Harold F. Peace. C. 1908/14.

16. 374 Red and pink roses,
539 Swans,
511 Boating lake.

374

539

511

679

273

419

17. 679 Des No 2438, the vase matches clock 783.
273 Des No 1907,
419 Des No 1907. The vase decorations show
the popular romantic influence of the desert
in the late 1920's.

18. A selection of vases
decorated with
Swans, a popular
Royal Bird and a Folk
Scene.

600   347   359   321

636

538

432

433

610

355

570

634

19. A selection of 9 small
vases
636 Spill vase Lovebirds,
432 Rural scene,
610 Robins,
634 Spill vase Lanterns,
538 Rural,
433 matches clock 433,
426 Des No 1760,
355 Swans,
570 Des No 2480.

426

20. *Lustre ware in the Napier shape, Des No 2337 Wash jug and bowl, chamber pot, toothbrush holder, large covered powder bowl, candlestick and 523 trinket tray.*

21. *1930's design wash set in the Silvo shape. Wash jug and bowl, chamber pot, toothbrush holder, 594 trinket tray, hair-baller ring stand, covered pot. Des No 2480.*

22. *Wash jug and bowl, chamber pot and soap dish on the Napier shape. Des No 2744.*

23. *Wash jug and bowl toothbrush holder, low covered pot hairballer, ring stand, covered pot, trinket tray all in Silvo shape. Cottage and lily pond.*

24. *Wash jug and bowl on the Napier shape in 'Scenes of The Old Country' Des No 2675.*

25. *Wash jug and bowl in the later 'Moonlight' design showing the moon and water. The bowl is a different shape and unmarked. Des No 2157.*

26. *A complete dressing table set on the Napier shape in black 'Moonlight' Des No 1500. Trinket tray, candlestick, large covered powder bowl, toothbrush holder, hair-baller, covered pot, ring tree, pintray, hatpin stand.*

27. *Dressing table sets, Silhouette Windmill and Lovebirds Des No 2007, showing the hexagonal/ octagonal shapes. See page 137 for the hair-baller. It is on three feet. Items at the bottom left to right, candlestick, covered pot, hand ring stand, hatpin stand, covered pot, candlestick, three covered pots. Note similarity to Noritaki. Theirs are smaller.*

28. *A selection of chamber pots: the two middle ones are marked Silvo, the top one being cellulose.*

29. *A rare shaving mug of a very distinctive design Mould No 484 Des No 1330.*

484

30. *Gothic set,*
   Des No 2495.

648   648   648

31. *Heart shape, Des No 2548.*

609   608   609

Roman   606   605   606   Roman

32. *5 piece set, Des No 2092.*

33. *Ploughing.*

511   520   511

34. *Bedroom set Des No 2099, (movement replaced).*

626   433   626

35. *Blue and Black 'Moonlight'. Des No 1500.*

650   649   650

36. Aerographed
and hand finished
in paint .

610   230   610

37. Clock 783 Moonlight,
(movement replaced).
Vase 678 matches this.
Clock 744 Hand painted
Dutch scene.

783   744

604

482

38. *Clock 604 Des No 2216.*
Vase 600 possibly
matches this.
Clock 482. Des No 1760,
(movement replaced).

39. *Clock 651 Des No 2436,*
(movement replaced).
Clock 651 "Scello' ware,
vase 652 matches
these.

651   651

832   862   832

40. *Egyptian, embossed, Reg No 774557 in cellulose see page 100*

650   649   650

41. *Part of the expanded range of the popular embossed Wild Duck pattern in cellulose. See Reg Nos pages 90 – 99 Refer to mould number list Nos 649, 650 for explanation on double use of numbers.*
The clock is not original and the vase on the right should have the duck flying inwards.

696 696 696

42. *This embossed cellulose set depicts a lady and gentleman meeting and walking in a garden.*

43. *A bedroom set of embossed 'Wild Duck' in cellulose. Refer to mould number list No 433 for explanation on double use of numbers.*

433 433 433

659   650   659

44. *This is an imitation blue
and white Wedgwood
with the pattern in relief.
It is marked 'Scello Ware'
and was also produced
in black and white. Refer
to backstamp pages 18
& 21*

575

958

NN

559

440

492

45. Centrepieces and rose
bowls, left to right starting at
the top.
575 Moonlight Des No 1500,
NN Country windmill,
440 Moonlight Des No 1500,
958 Harvest Poppy,
559 Moonlight Des No 1500,
492 Red Rose Des No 1760.

46. 654 Sandwich tray,
675 Wall plate,
Tea plate NN Blue
'Moonlight' Des No 1500.

675

654

NN

893

NN

127

302

603

NN

47. Six Jardinieres.
893 Swans,
NN Butterfly & House Des No 2096,
127 Silhouette Windmill,
302 Arabian Des No 1907,
603 Cottage Garden Des No 2795,
NN Red Rose Des No 1760.

48. 262 Blue Iris Des No 2139.

262

185   262   315   362

49. Jardinieres.
185 Swans,
315 Swans
262 Family and Farm by
Harold F. Peace,
362 Hunting.

50. NN Rural Scenes.

NN

51. 563 Swans,
NN large size Des No 1682,
Silvo size 1 Alpine Boy and G
563 Farm buildings,
NN Shrimping,
Silvo size 3 Floral spray.

563   563   NN   NN   NN   NN

560   *NN*   *NN*

52. *560 Blue Iris Des*
No1949,
NN Cream Jug Arab
Travellers Des No 2604,
NN Pink Roses.

53. *573 Des No 2714,*
NN Twisted flute
Silhouette Harbour,
666 Des No 1392.

573   *NN*   *666*

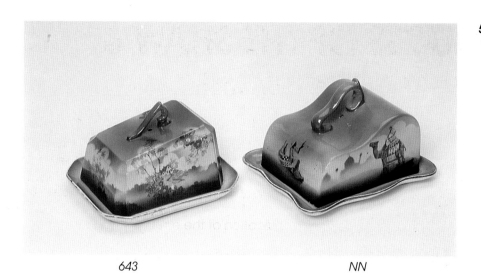

54. Cheese dishes
643 Cottage Garden
Des No 2795,
NN Camel and rider.

643   *NN*

55. 666 'Scenes of the Old
Country.'

666

Chapter 6

THE PRODUCTS OF THE SHAW & COPESTAKE FACTORY - II

CELLULOSE HOLLOW WARE

Towards the end of the 1920's the factory began to turn away from the older style of ware and to look for new products. Richard Hull Jnr was undoubtedly the driving force. His travels in Europe and the colonies enabled him to bring back many ideas. He was particularly keen on animals and novelty items and his enthusiasm is attested to by the explosion of mould numbers from 1931/2 onwards: all manner of weird and wonderful shapes began to appear on a receptive, and sometimes astonished, market.

In 1928 or 1929 the factory began to use the cellulose paint finish. This was a new way of finishing biscuit ware (as undecorated ware was known) which was both cheap and highly decorative. The base coats were applied by either dipping or aerographing (spraying) the biscuit ware with all other colour and highlights being painted by hand. Most items were given a semi-gloss varnish for protection.

The first range to be given this treatment was the embossed Lord and Lady Walking in a Garden, closely followed by the Wild Duck range which started in August 1931, to be followed next year by the Egyptian range.
The factory was particularly proud of these patterns, so much so that they incorporated them in their headed stationery:

SHAW & COPESTAKE
SYLVAN WORKS, LONGTON, STAFFS., ENGLAND

MANUFACTURERS OF
EGYPTIAN WARE
WILD DUCK WARE, ETC.

BUY BRITISH POTTERY

The Wild Duck range was particularly prolific, having at least twenty different items, many with their own registered design number. In the registered design section on page 90 – 99 can be seen a wash jug and bowl, trinket tray and other items which now appear for the first time in any published work. The shapes guide on page 122 – 126 give some indication of the enormous range.

See illustrations pages 54,55,65.

CELLULOSE FIGURES, ANIMALS & NOVELTIES

Figurines are a relatively recent discovery and the number of new finds continues to grow. Covent Garden, Flower Sellers, Dancing Ladies, Gnomes and Little Red Riding Hood are examples of the range. They come in sizes from "5 & 8" tall and are all hand painted. The early "Dogs" are a little crude by later standards, but the "Toby Jugs" are, by contrast, very finely modelled.

For many collectors the essence of Shaw & Copestake is the humour which crept into the modelling from about 1931, with top hats on birds and bow ties on cats starting to make an appearance. These were expanded and elaborated under the SylvaC name in later years. See Illustrations 73 & 74

ART DECO STYLE WARE

Around the mid 1930's the new matt glaze began to be used alongside the cellulose paint. These finishes were used on what Shaw & Copestake called "up-to-date shapes" what we would today call "Art Deco". This last of the truly sumptuous style of applied arts, covering everything from furniture and buildings to tableware was nowhere more pronounced than in the field of ceramics.

Its origins go back much further than is commonly supposed and was partly a reaction to the fussiness of Art Nouveau. It was in full swing by the early decades of the 20th century.

Shaw & Copestake had little to do with the early Arts and Crafts movement which was primarily responsible for Art Deco, but like many manufacturers were greatly influenced by the new art forms. By the late 1920's and early 1930's the factory's Art Deco output was at full strength and many designs unique to Shaw & Copestake were being produced. Some of the many notable designs are illustrated on pages 76 – 80.

Old advertisement for Egyptian ware

785   1860   784

805

56. *Wild Duck. 1860 was a later addition to range.*

57. *703 Named 'Mikado' because they remind me of the Gilbert and Sullivan operas that were so fashionable   at the time.*

703   703

905   848   905

58. Harvest Poppy not
registered but exclusive
to Shaw and Copestake.

59. Carnation pattern Reg
No 790615 but later
called Cornflower.

977   974   967

60. *1008 Vase*
1001 Jug
Colourful floral designs.

1008   1001

61. *1075 Vase*
1078 Flower jug
Both in raised pattern with ribbing to
simulate hand-turned pottery.

1075   1078

1196   1138

62. 1196 Goblin jug, Reg No
    809115. see page 107
    1138 Stork jug.
    These items will be familiar
    to most collectors but
    perhaps not in the rare
    hand painted cellulose
    finish.

919   920   931   881

63. *These are hand painted and are produced in variety of colour combinations. Some occur in matt glaze.*

64. *Hand painted boy and girl Covent Garden flower sellers. These are posy vases having hollow tops.*

855   847

888   890   889

65. *Hand painted ladies in period dress.*

1033

66. *Hand painted Indian Chief.*

1081

67. Little Red Ridinghood.

1230   1231

68. *A pair of toby jugs.*
1230, Sarah Gamp in
matt glaze,
1231, Sam Weller hand
painted cellulose.

69. *Hand painted Gnomes.*
No 87 was part of the
later and separately
numbered series.

962   1024   1093   87

752   733   743

70. Part of an early
series of animals
and novelties.
Note the pelican is
wearing a top hat.

71. 700 Kingfisher on
flower stand in
bowl 726.
787 Flying Duck on
flower stand in
bowl 786,
1039 Kingfisher
vase in bowl 436,
They are all
aerographed and
hand painted.

700/726   1039/436   787/786

991   823   822/819

72. *991 Lion,*
      823 Lion with vase,
      822 using lion 819.

73. *845 Goblin/Lepricorn*
      with vase,
      843 Laughing cat.

845   843

788

1153

815

74. *815 Small elephant,*
788 Elephant with howdah,
1153 Elephant vase.
Elephants in black cellulose
were probably the first
successful range of animals
judging by the number of
different models
produced.

75. *Owl with tree trunk*
vase.

1004

76. 1375 Duck,
1326 Vase,
1327 Posy Holder,
1353 Posy holder
Reg No 823082, see
page 111
1466 Lizard,
1420 'Lucky Pixie'.

1375   1326   1327

1353   1466   1420

77. 1173 Vase,
1272 Vase,
1070 Jug,
1275 Vase,
1198 Watercress dish
and stand.

1173   1272   1070

1275   1198

829

1114

1125

1363

78. *829 Egyptian Jug Reg No 774557, see page 100 matt finish but also made in cellulose.*
1125 Bacchanti flower jug,
1114 Hollyhock flower iua.
1363 Cider jug.

1190   1167   1370   1318   1305   1116

79. 1167 Stag jug,
1318 Bunny jug,
1116 Dragon jug,
1190 Monkey Nut,
1370 Budgerigar jug,
1305 Birds Nest.

80. *1384 Wall vase,*
1226 Clown,
1385 Wall vase.

1384   1226   1385

81. *1340 Yacht Reg No 826482,*
1352 posy holder Reg No 823084, see page 113
1307 Rope Range vase,
1289 Miniature character jug,
1402 Flying duck,
1337 Flower Lady.

1340   1289   1352   1307
                           1402   1337

902   489   1148

82. 902 Ginger jar,
     489 Bowl,
     1148 Vase.

Pieces of deco ware with oxide drip glazes put on top of
blue or brown base glaze. This ran when fired producing
an unusual and fine contempory decoration.

83. 1345 Vase,
     1341 Vase/mug.
     Another technique used
     in the 1930's with running
     glazes to give an abstract
     marbled affect.

1345   1341

Chapter 7

REGISTERED DESIGN NUMBERS
With photographs of the original designs

Design registration lasted five years and on application could be extended for a further five and then again for a final five years.

Registered By Shaw and Copestake

Vase	628381	19th Nov 1913
Vase	630194	1st Jan 1914
Vase	633217	4th Mar 1914
Vase	634174	21st Mar 1914
Vase	635698	21st Apr 1914
Venetian design	716616	15th Oct 1925
Lovebirds design	716616	registered by James Davis, Berry Works, off Stafford St, Longton. Stoke on Trent. – expired 1930.

Registered by William Shaw and Richard Hull T/A S&C

Sydney Harbour Bridge Clock	758626	14th Oct 1930 Bridge opened 1932
Wild Duck	762858 jardiniere	August 1931
Wild Duck	768168 oval vase	13th Oct 1931
Wild Duck	768695 round vase	17th Nov1931
Wild Duck	768696 clock	17th Nov 1931
Wild Duck	769027 diamond shaped tray	2nd Dec 1931
Wild Duck	769028 candlestick	2nd Dec1931
Wild Duck	769029 dia shape Trinket box	2nd Dec 1931
Wild Duck	769285 oval vase	11th Dec 1931
Wild Duck	769699 dia shape wash jug	4th Jan 1932
Wild Duck	769725 wash bowl	6th Jan 1932
Egyptian scene	774557 design only	27th June 1932
'Story book'	778220 vase	14th Nov 1932

Dog Mac sitting	778504	25th Nov 1932

The above model was registered by Otakar Steinberger (Czechoslovak subject) 142 Queens Rd, Peckham, London, and bought by S&C.

Footballer	787779	11th Nov 1933
Carnation	790615 vase	23rd Feb 1934
Corkscrew cat	806569	18th Sept 1935
Monkey Nut	809067 flower jug	15th Jan 1936
Mushroom Gnome	809115 flower jug	17th Jan 1936
Dog glum sitting	813261	24th Jun 1936
Rabbit lop ear	815839	16th Oct 1936

Registered by Shaw and Copestake Ltd

Hare 'Harry'	815840	16th Oct 1936
Deco posy holder	823082	2nd Sept 1937
Seagull on wave	823083	2nd Sept 1937
Deco posy holder	823084	2nd Sept 1937
Yacht	826482	24th Feb 1938
Top hat and cat	833892	7th Mar 1939
Duck	833893	7th Mar 1939

Original Design No. 628381 November 1913 – Illustration Page 36

Original Design No. 630194 January 1914

Original Design No. 633217 March 1914 – Illustration Page 26

Original Design No.634174 March 1914

Original Design No 635698 April 1914

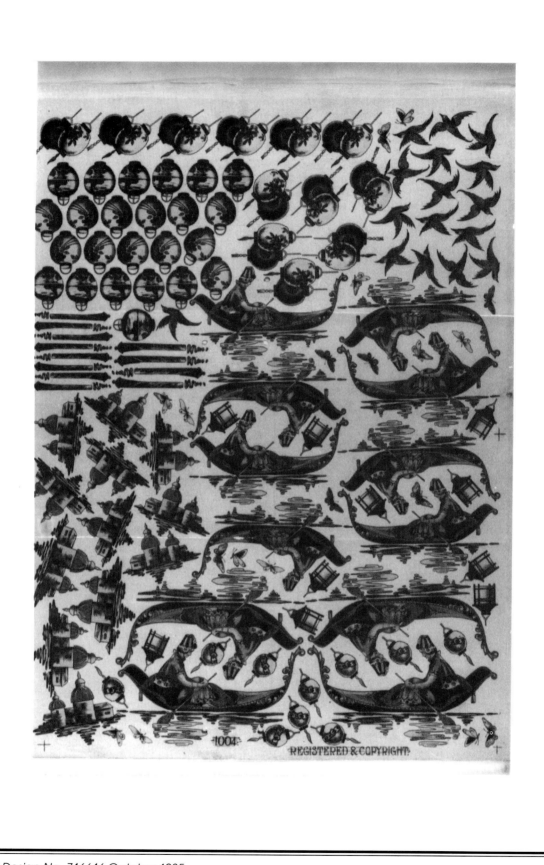

Original Design No. 716616 October 1925

758626

FRONT
VIEW

SIDE
PERSPECTIVE
VIEW.

Original Design No. 758626 October 1930

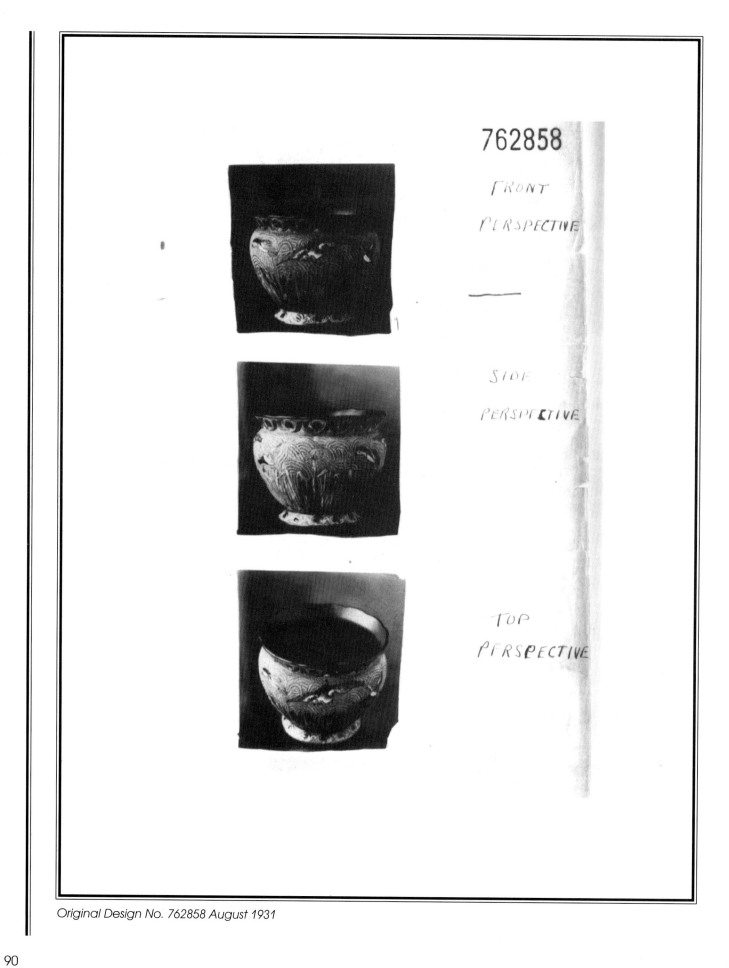

762858

FRONT
PERSPECTIVE

SIDE
PERSPECTIVE

TOP
PERSPECTIVE

Original Design No. 762858 August 1931

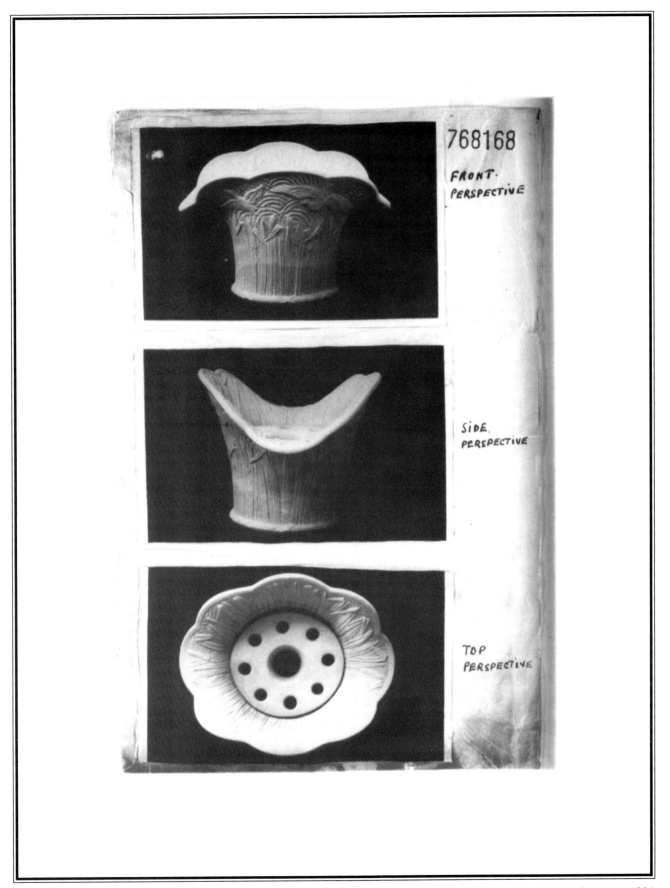

768168

FRONT. PERSPECTIVE

SIDE. PERSPECTIVE

TOP PERSPECTIVE

Original Design No. 768168 October 1931

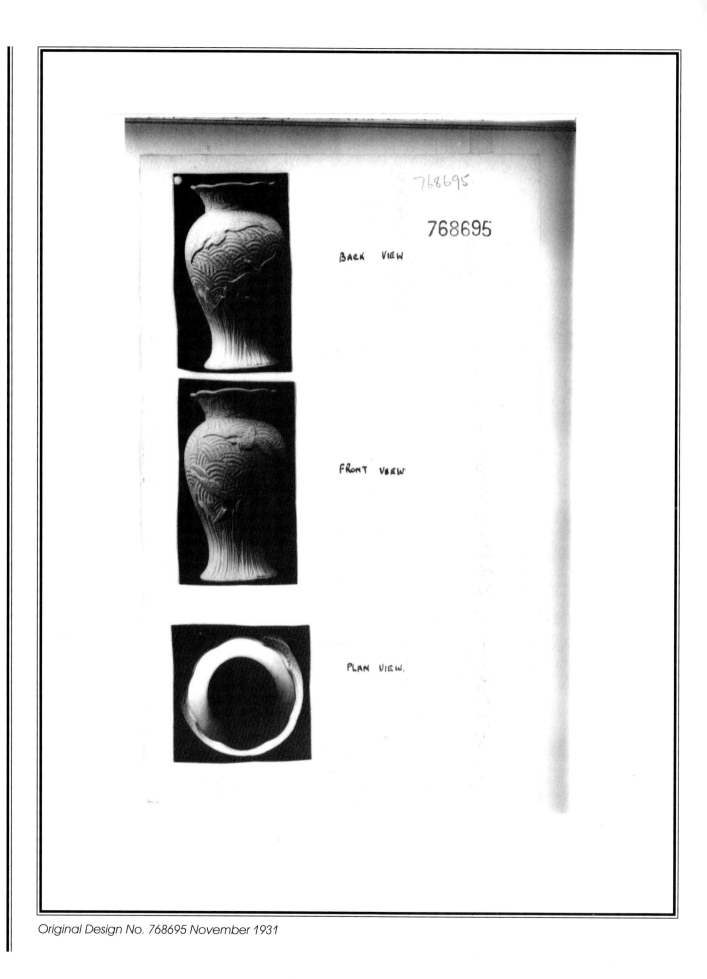

768695

768695

BACK VIEW

FRONT VIEW

PLAN VIEW.

Original Design No. 768695 November 1931

768696

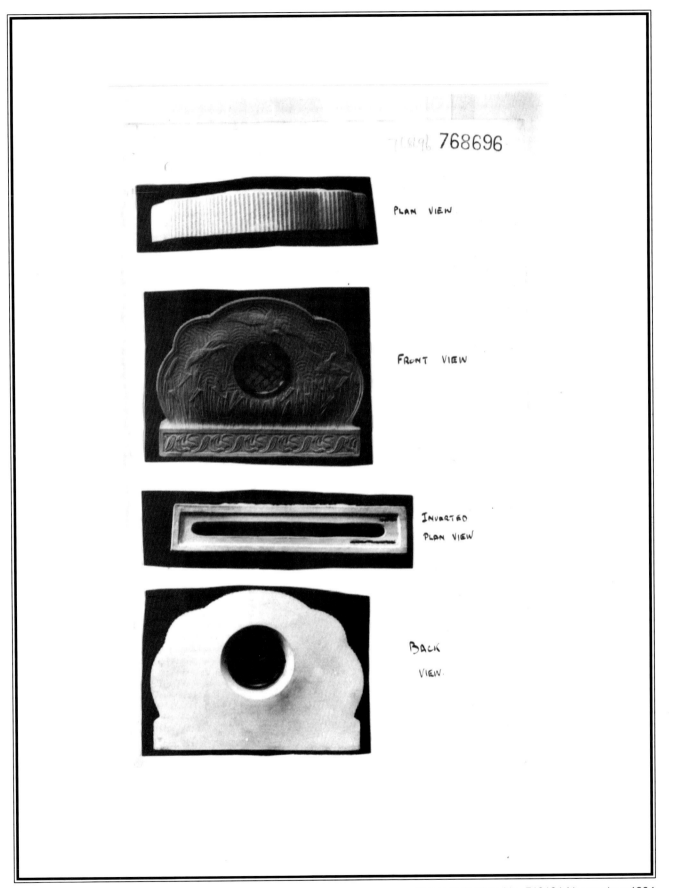

PLAN VIEW

FRONT VIEW

INVERTED
PLAN VIEW

BACK
VIEW.

Original Design No. 768696 November 1931

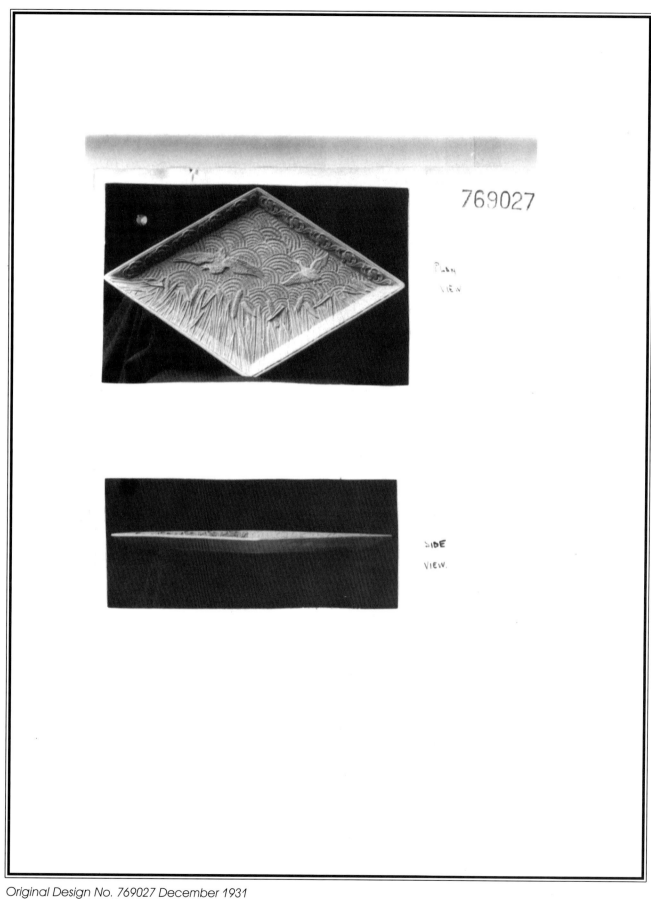

769027

PLAN
VIEW

SIDE
VIEW.

Original Design No. 769027 December 1931

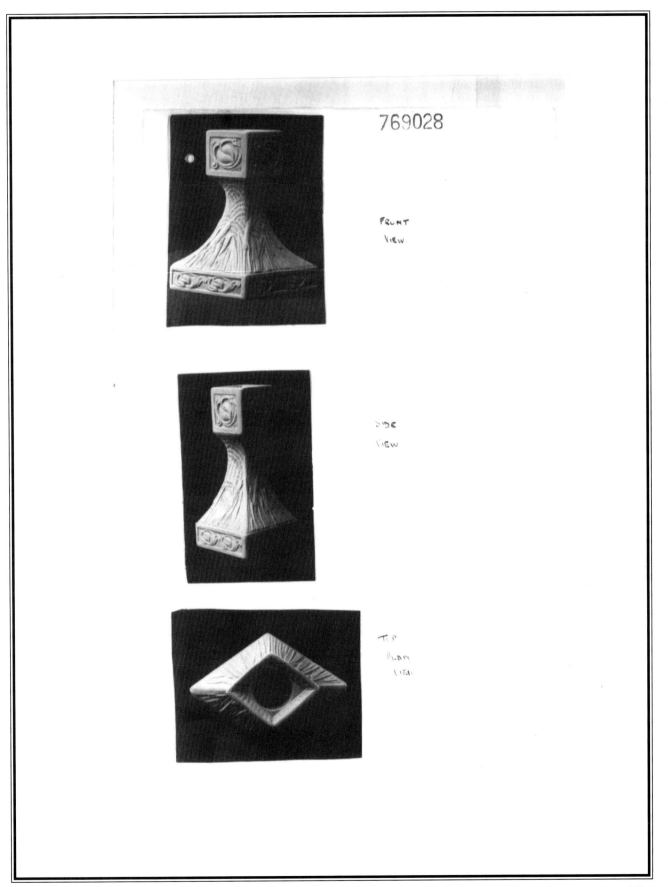

769028

FRONT
VIEW.

SIDE
VIEW

TOP
PLAN
VIEW

Original Design No. 769028 December 1931

95

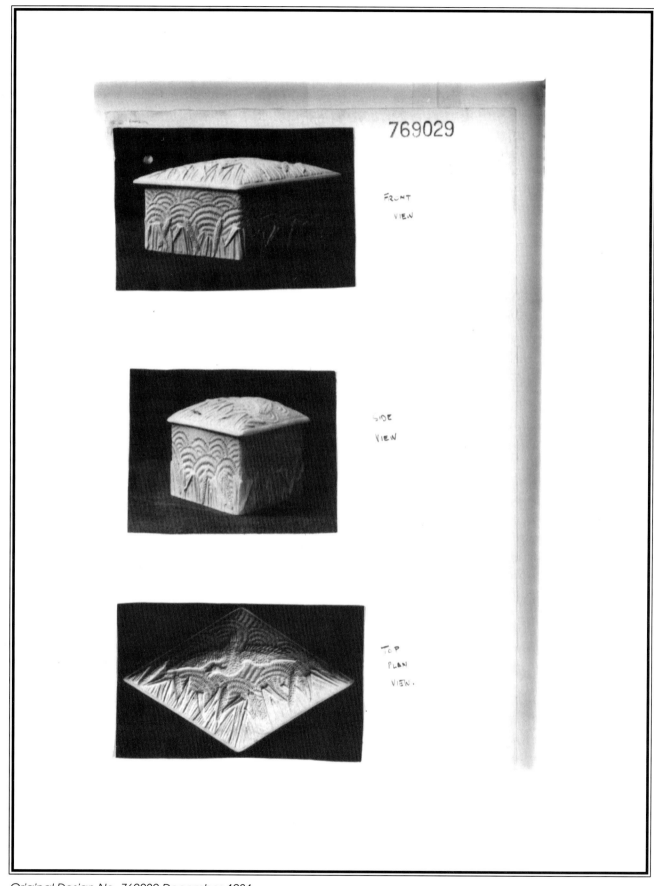

769029

FRONT
VIEW

SIDE
VIEW

TOP
PLAN
VIEW.

Original Design No. 769029 December 1931

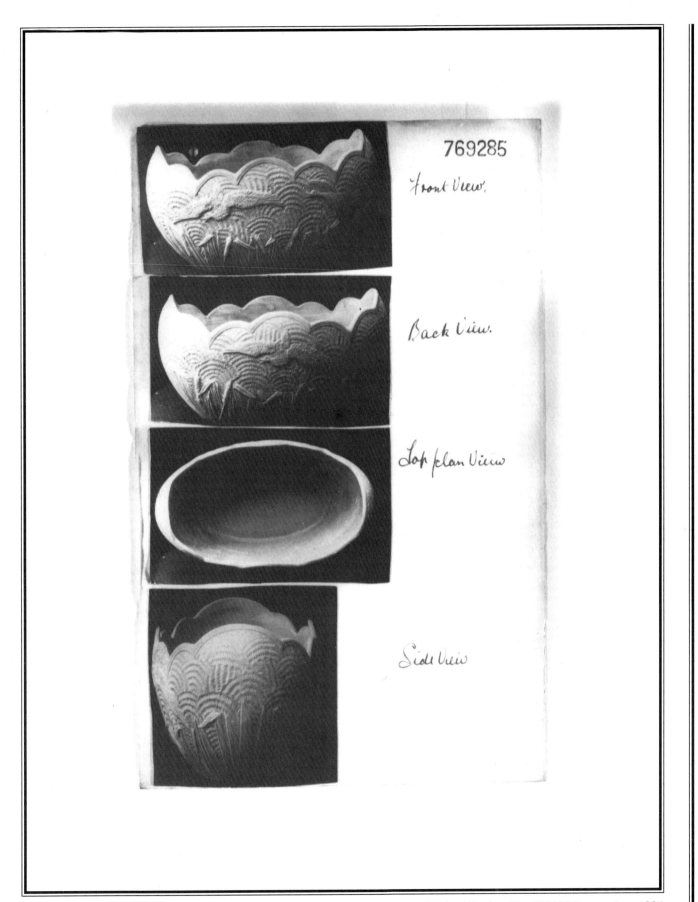

769285

Front View.

Back View.

Top plan View

Side View

Original Design No. 769285 December 1931

769699

Front View

Back View

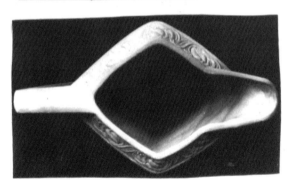

Top Plan View

Original Design No. 769699 January 1932

769725

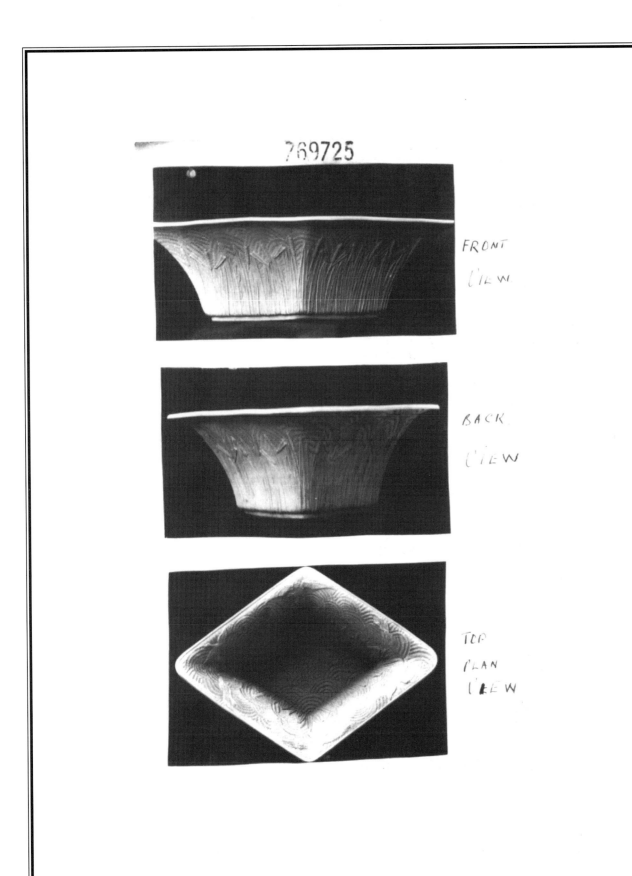

FRONT
VIEW

BACK
VIEW

TOP
PLAN
VIEW

Original Design No. 769725

774557

774557

DEVELOPED VIEW OF PATTERN.

~~SHAPE OF VASE~~
SIDE VIEW OF. VASE

Original Design No. 774557 June 1932

778220

Developed View of Pattern

Front View of Vase.

Back View of Vase.

778504

Original Design 778504 November 1932

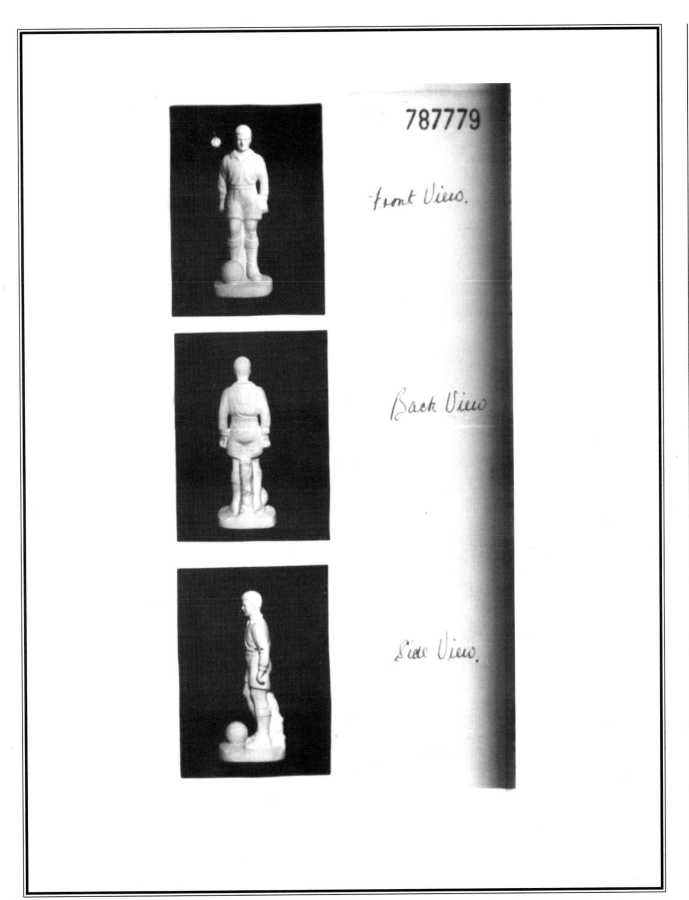

787779

Front View.

Back View.

Side View.

Original Design No. 787779 November 1933

103

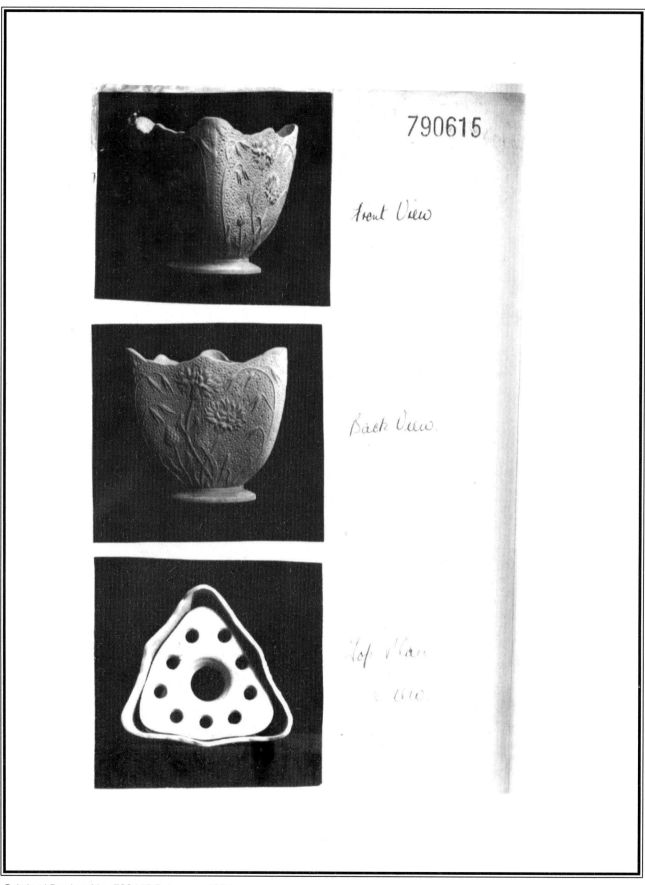

790615

Front View

Back View

Top Plan
View

Original Design No. 790615 February 1934

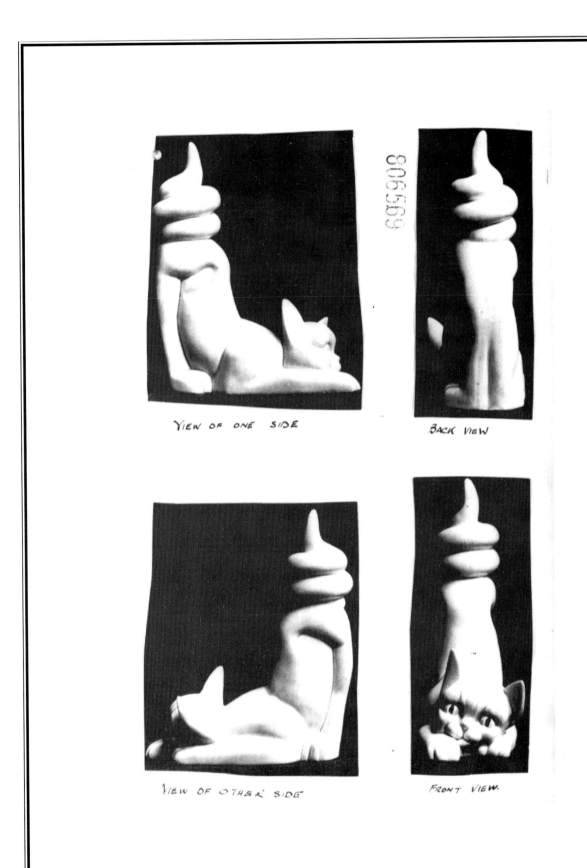

VIEW OF ONE SIDE

BACK VIEW

VIEW OF OTHER SIDE

FRONT VIEW.

Original Design No. 806569 September 1935

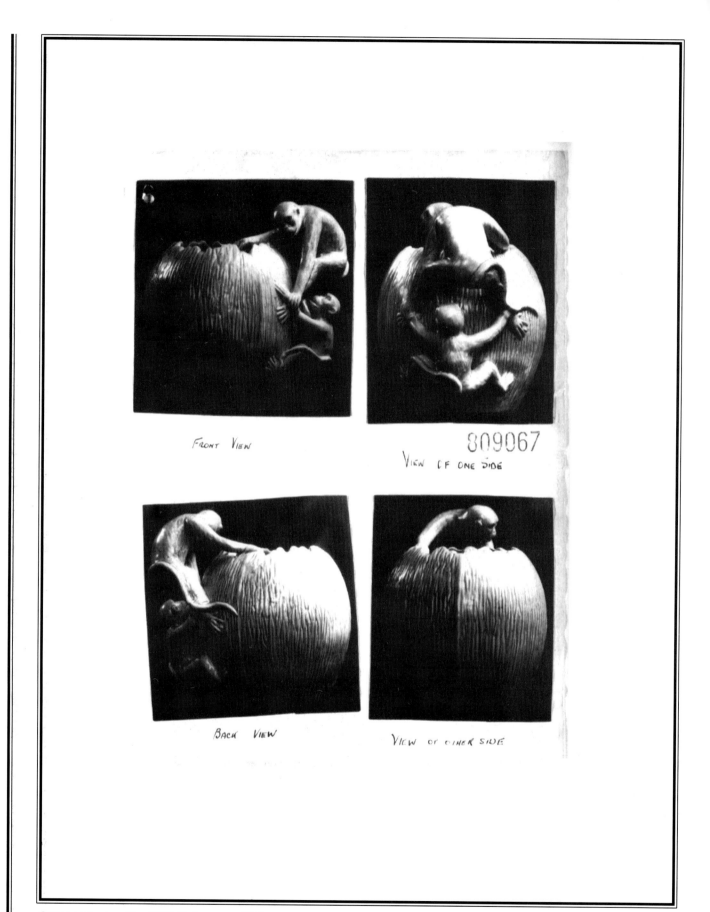

FRONT VIEW

VIEW OF ONE SIDE

809067

BACK VIEW

VIEW OF OTHER SIDE

Original Design No. 809067 January 1936

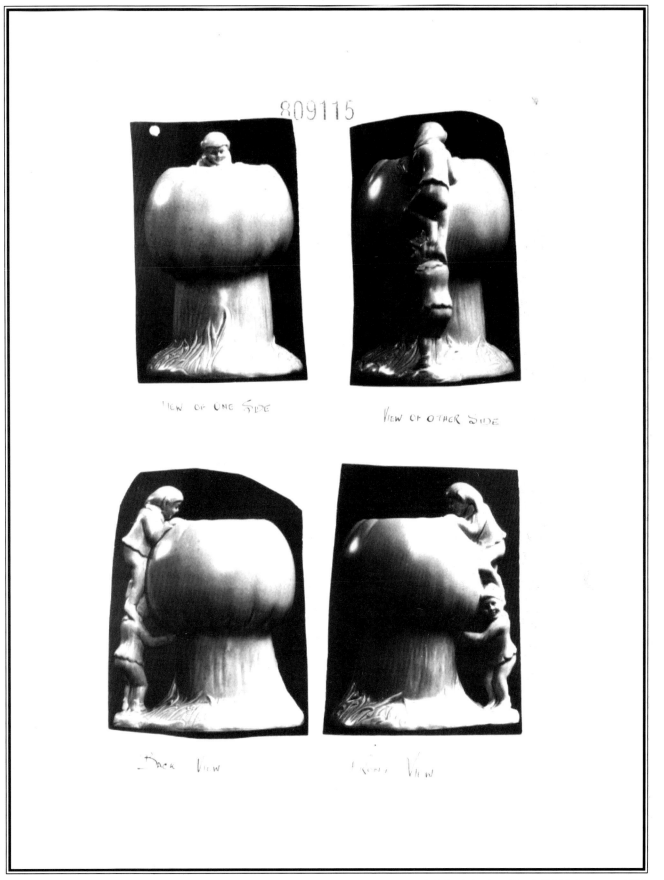

809115

VIEW OF ONE SIDE

VIEW OF OTHER SIDE

BACK VIEW

FRONT VIEW

Original Design No. 809115 January 1936

813261

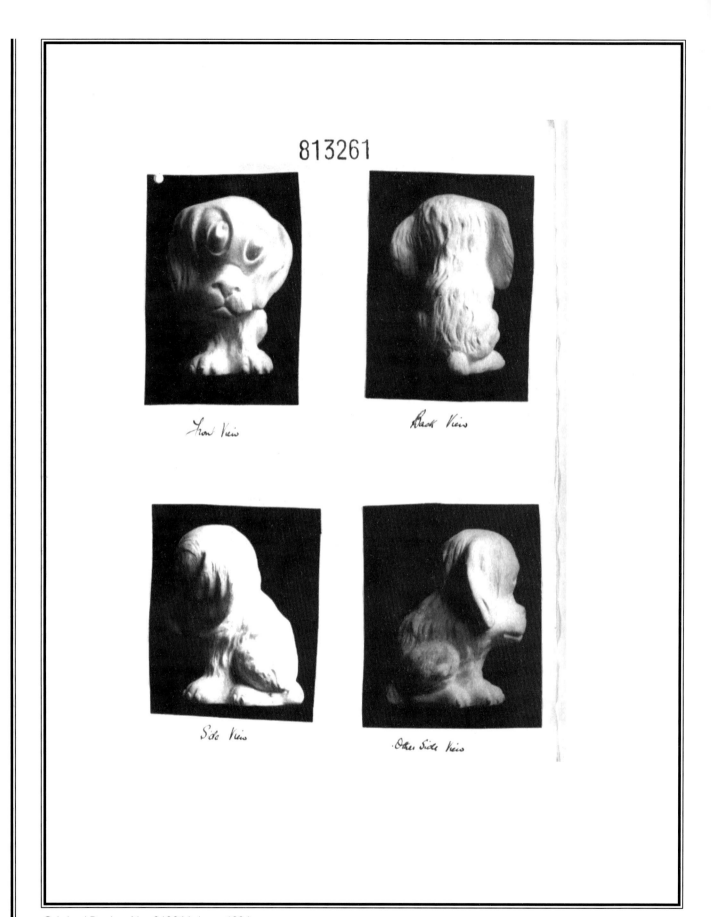

Front View

Back View

Side View

Other Side View

Original Design No. 813261 June 1936

815839

BACK VIEW   FRONT VIEW

VIEW OF ONE SIDE   VIEW OF OTHER SIDE

Original Design No. 815839

815840

FRONT VIEW.

SIDE VIEW.

Original Design No. 815840 October 1936

823082

SIDE VIEW.

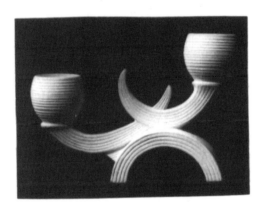

FRONT VIEW.

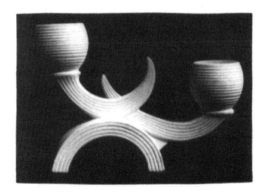

BACK VIEW.

Original Design No. 823082 September 1937

823083

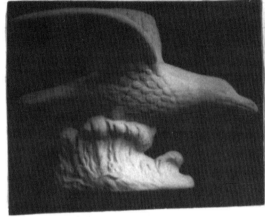

FRONT VIEW

BACK VIEW.

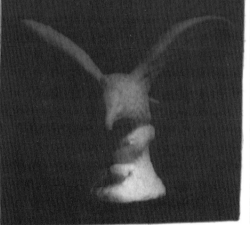

Original Design No. 823083 September 1937

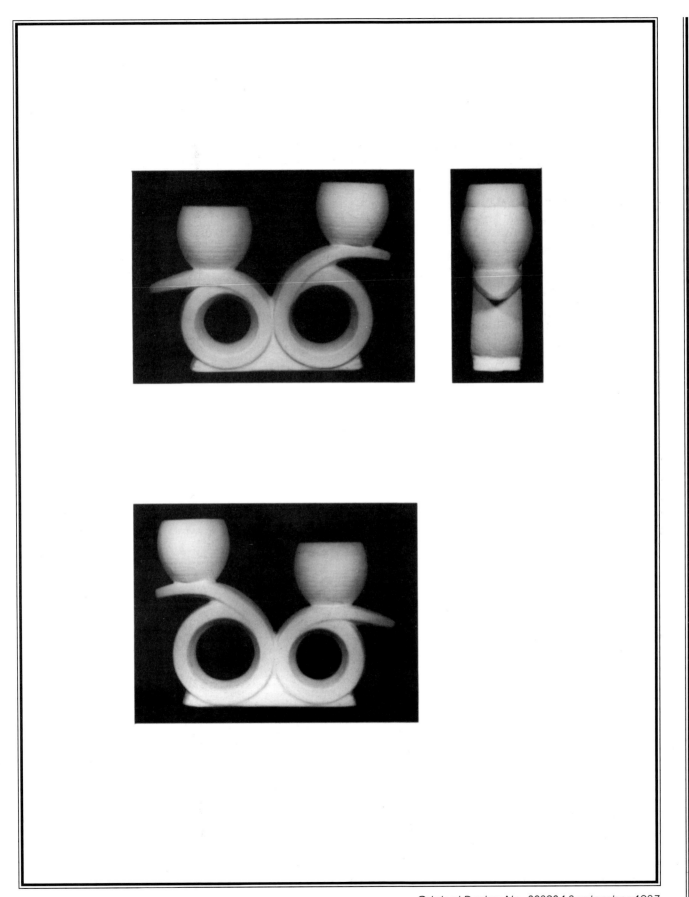

Original Design No. 823084 September 1937

113

826482

FRONT VIEW

SIDE VIEW

BACK VIEW

Original Design No. 826482 February 1938

833892

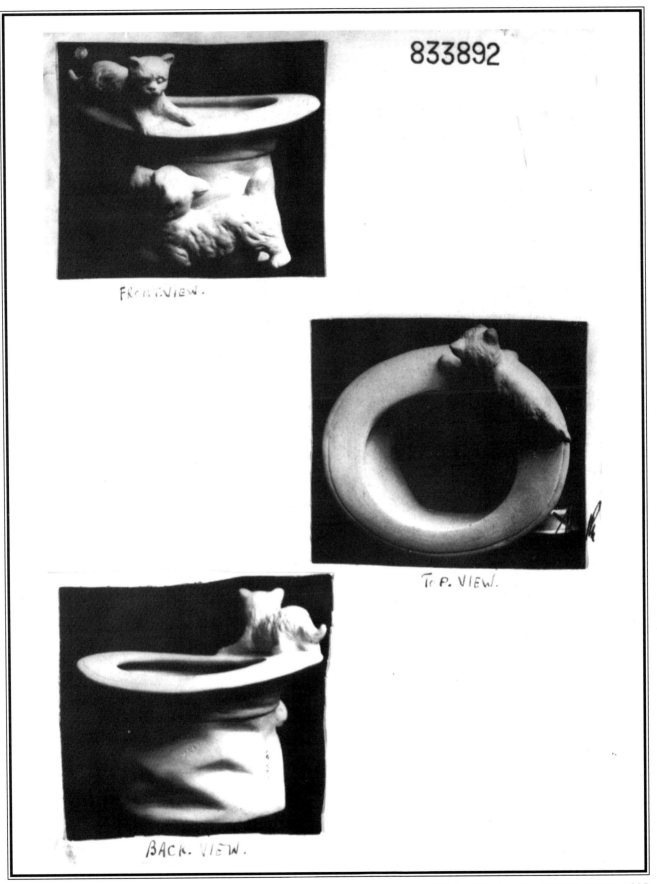

FRONT VIEW.

TOP. VIEW.

BACK. VIEW.

Original Design No. 833892 March 1939

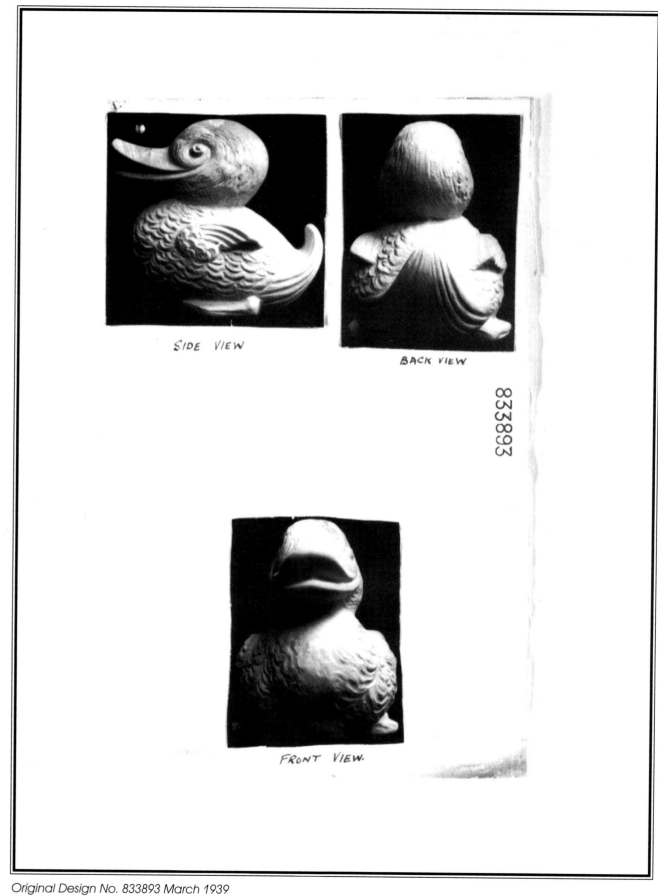

SIDE VIEW

BACK VIEW

833893

FRONT VIEW.

Original Design No. 833893 March 1939

Chapter 8

SHAPE GUIDE

These are outline drawings of the basic mould shape in numerical order. This will help to clarify some of the early shapes and numbers and identify Shaw and Copestake moulds or shapes from other manufacturers. Unfortunately the list does not contain all the known shapes, but lists those to which I have had access. I hope to be able to continue these at a later stage.

Drawings not to scale

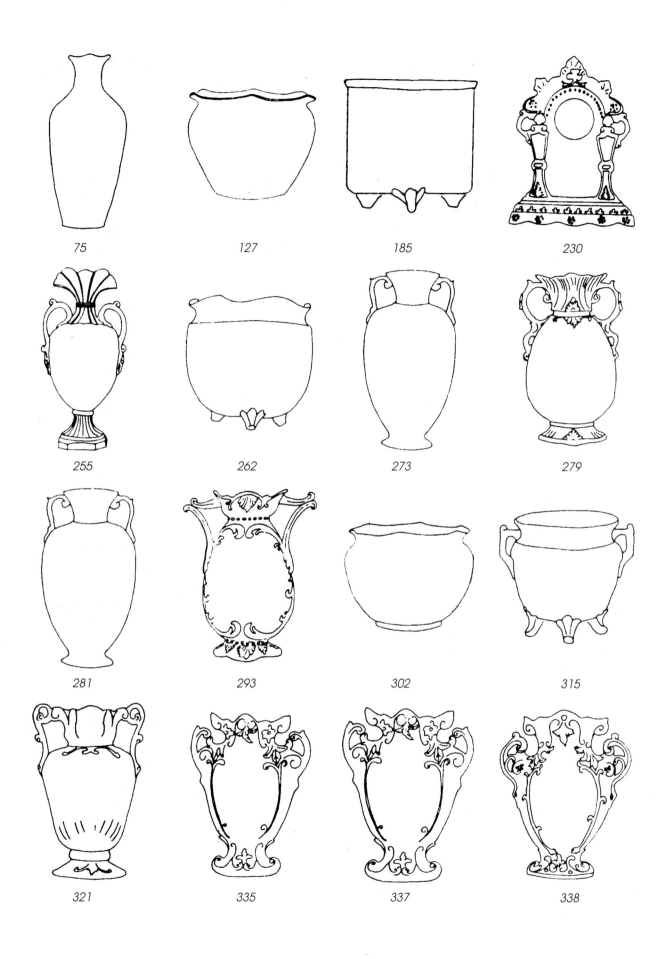

75

127

185

230

255

262

273

279

281

293

302

315

321

335

337

338

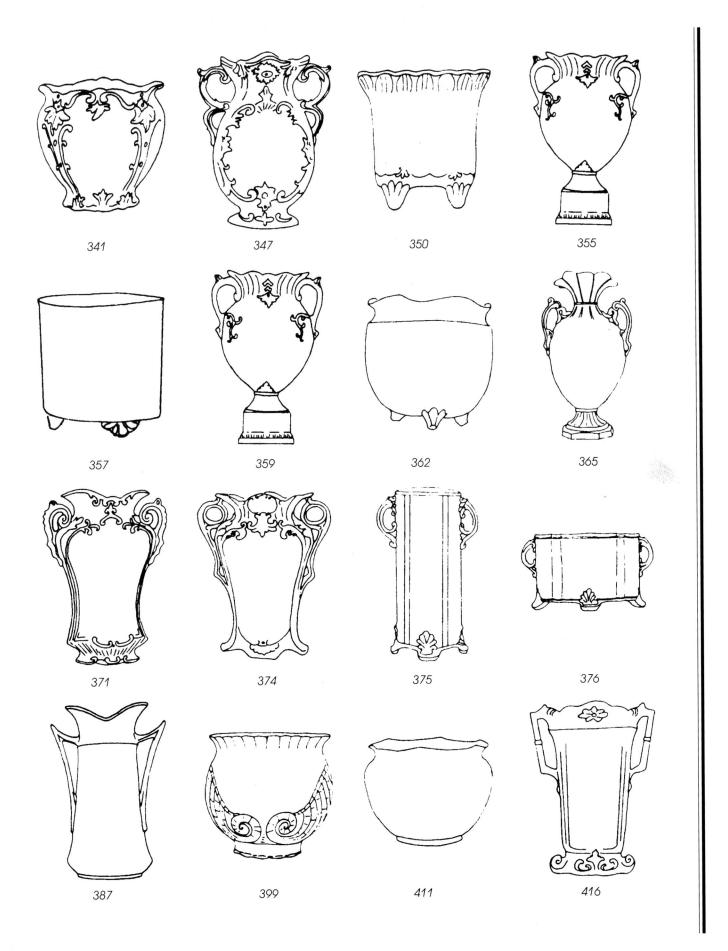

341   347   350   355

357   359   362   365

371   374   375   376

387   399   411   416

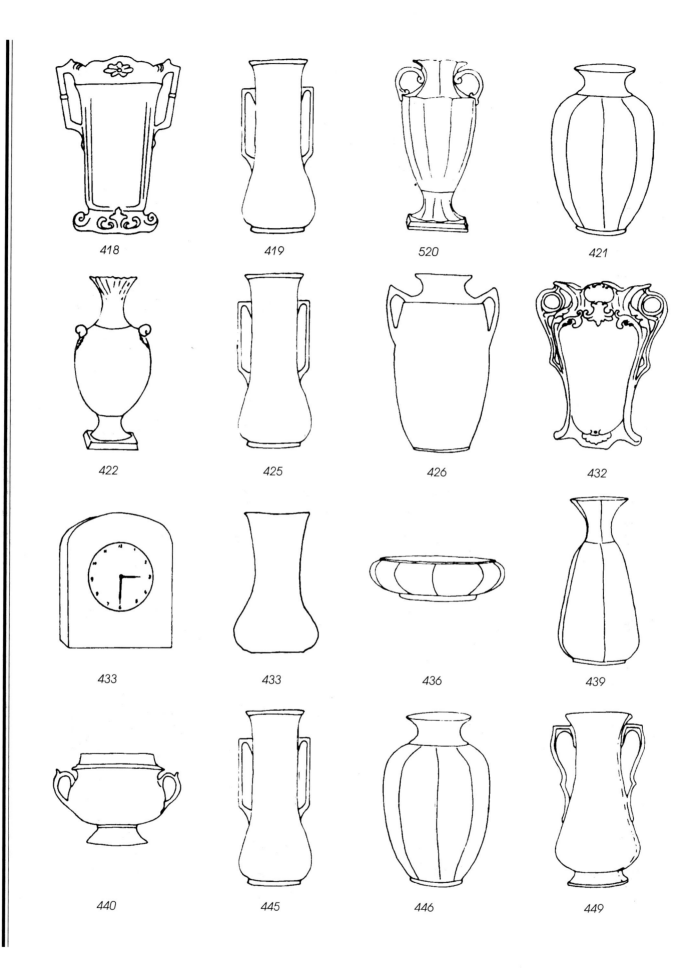

418

419

520

421

422

425

426

432

433

433

436

439

440

445

446

449

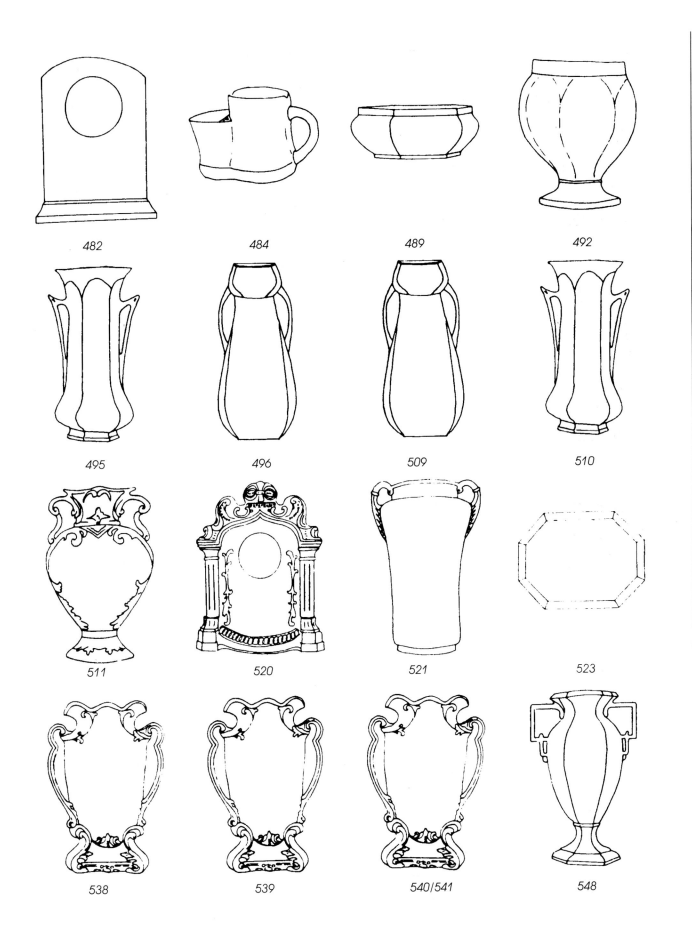

482

484

489

492

495

496

509

510

511

520

521

523

538

539

540/541

548

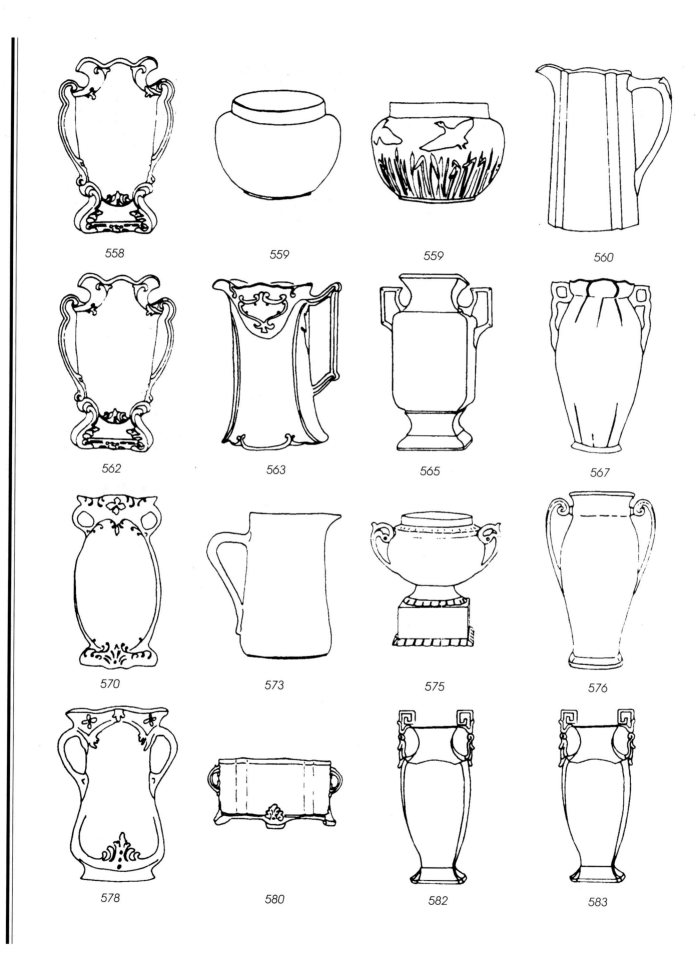

558

559

559

560

562

563

565

567

570

573

575

576

578

580

582

583

587   594   600   603

604   605   606   608

608   609   610   613

614   622   626   627

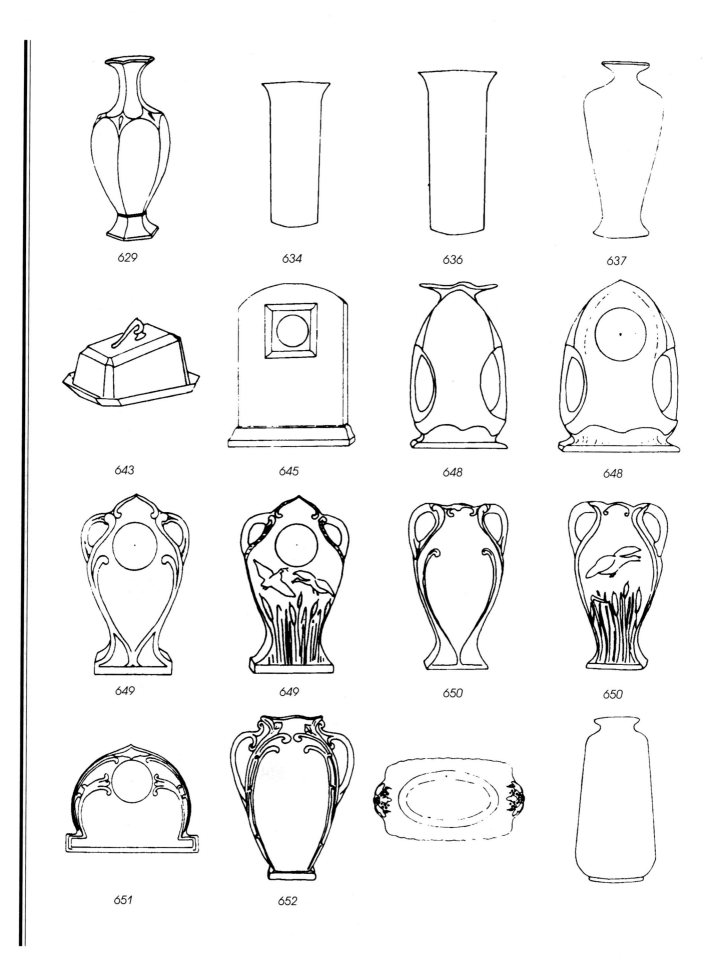

629

634

636

637

643

645

648

648

649

649

650

650

651

652

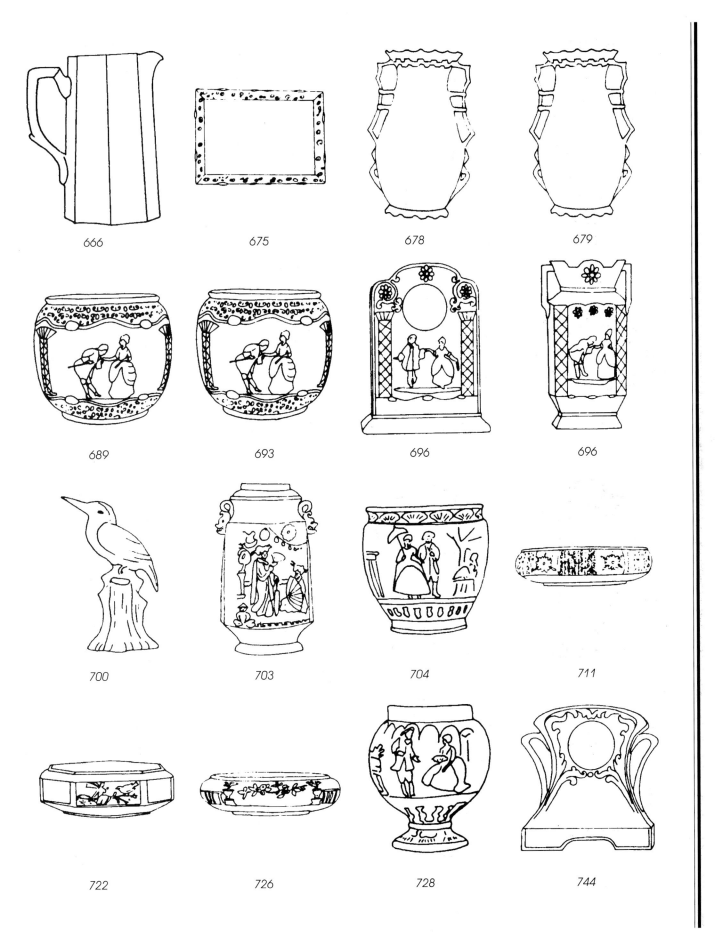

666

675

678

679

689

693

696

696

700

703

704

711

722

726

728

744

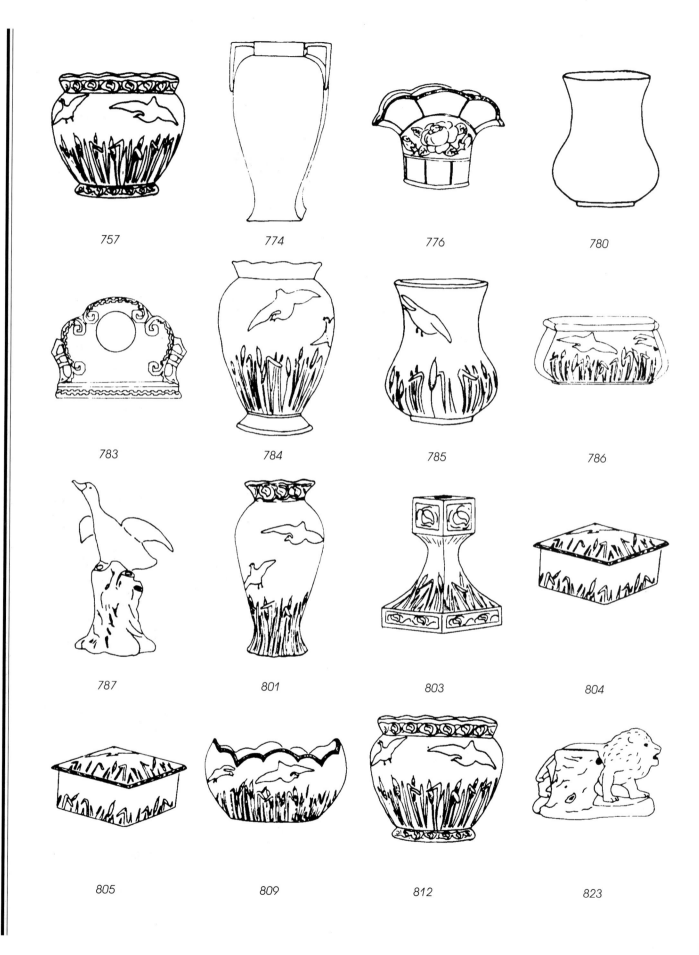

757

774

776

780

783

784

785

786

787

801

803

804

805

809

812

823

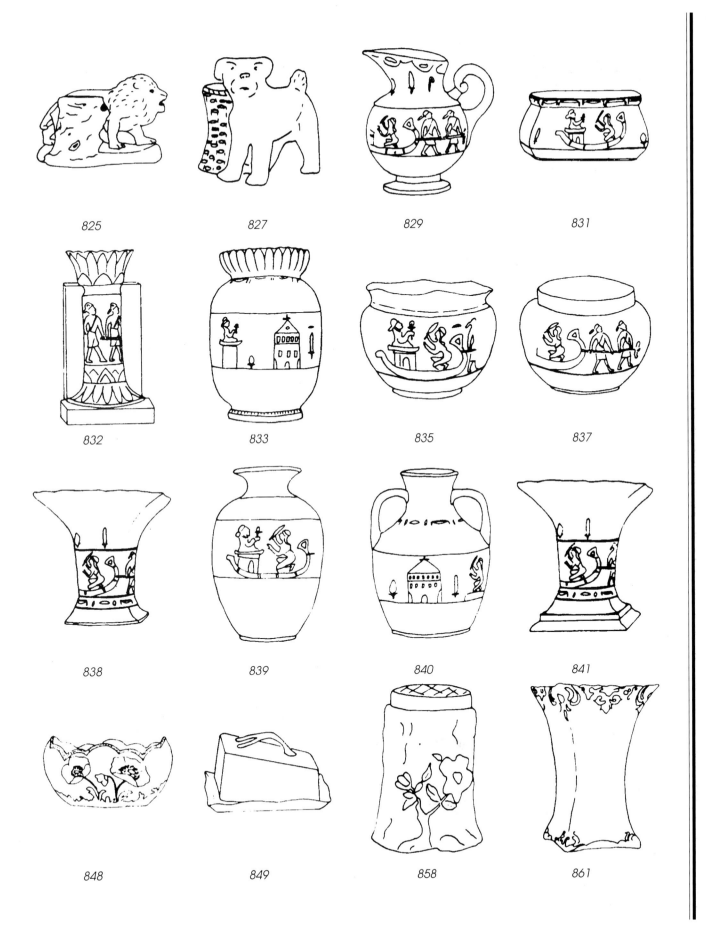

825   827   829   831

832   833   835   837

838   839   840   841

848   849   858   861

862

886

893

898

902

903

905

926

944

945

958

964

967

974

977

1001

1002

1004

1007

1008

1011

1014

1039

1070

1071

1075

1078

1090

1091

1109

1111

1113

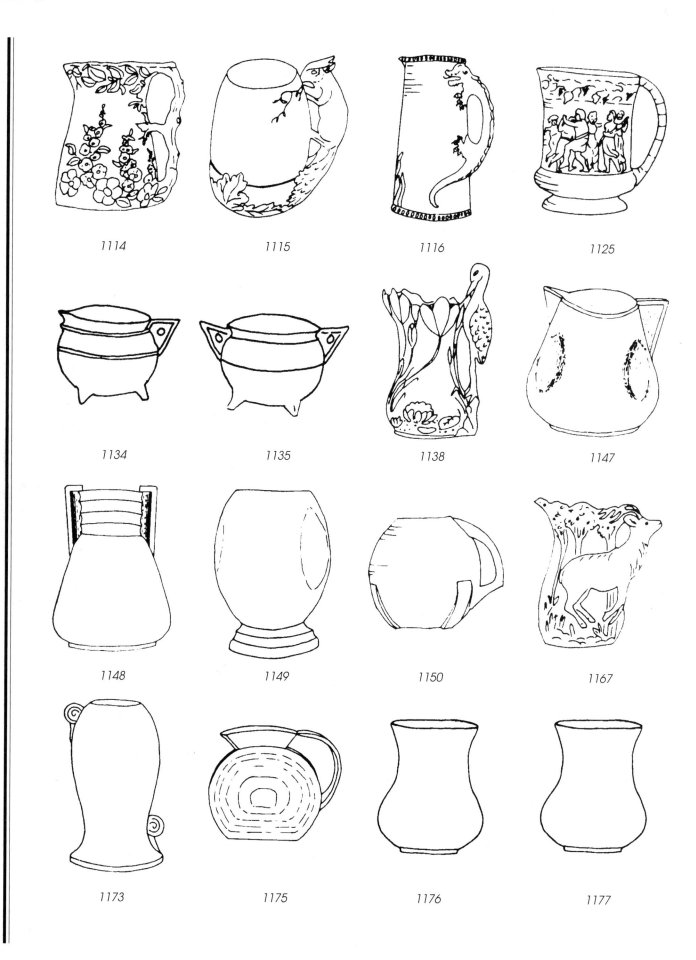

1114

1115

1116

1125

1134

1135

1138

1147

1148

1149

1150

1167

1173

1175

1176

1177

1178

1183

1184

1187

1189

1190

1195

1196

1198

1201

1202

1212

1213

1214

1215

1216

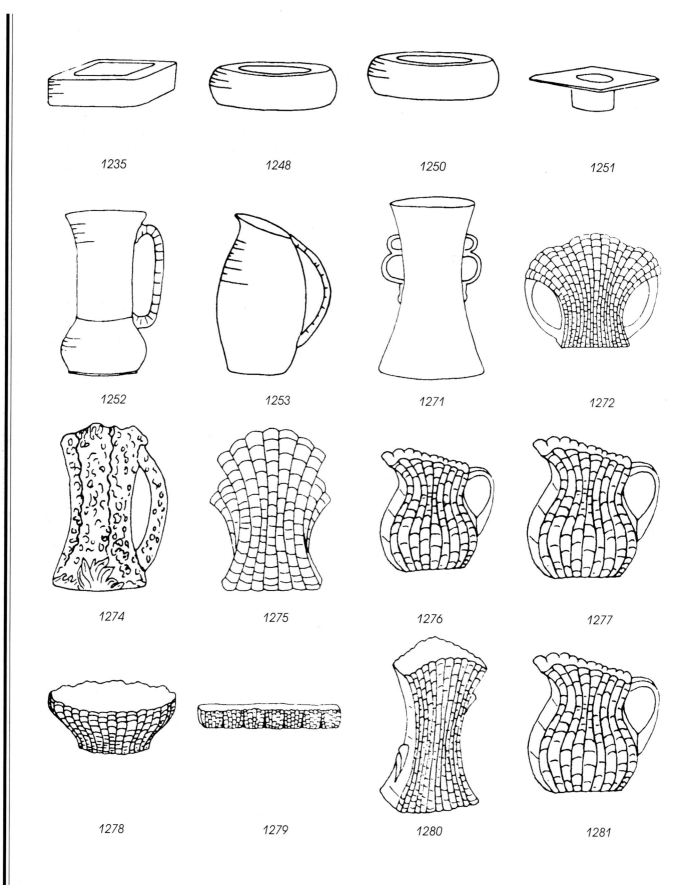

1235   1248   1250   1251

1252   1253   1271   1272

1274   1275   1276   1277

1278   1279   1280   1281

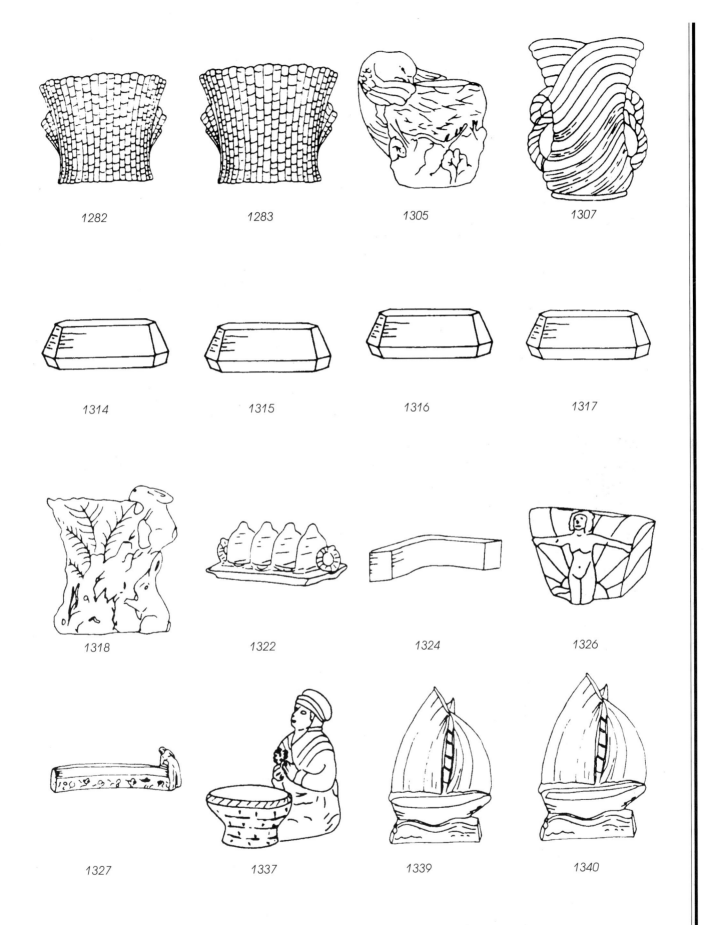

1282   1283   1305   1307

1314   1315   1316   1317

1318   1322   1324   1326

1327   1337   1339   1340

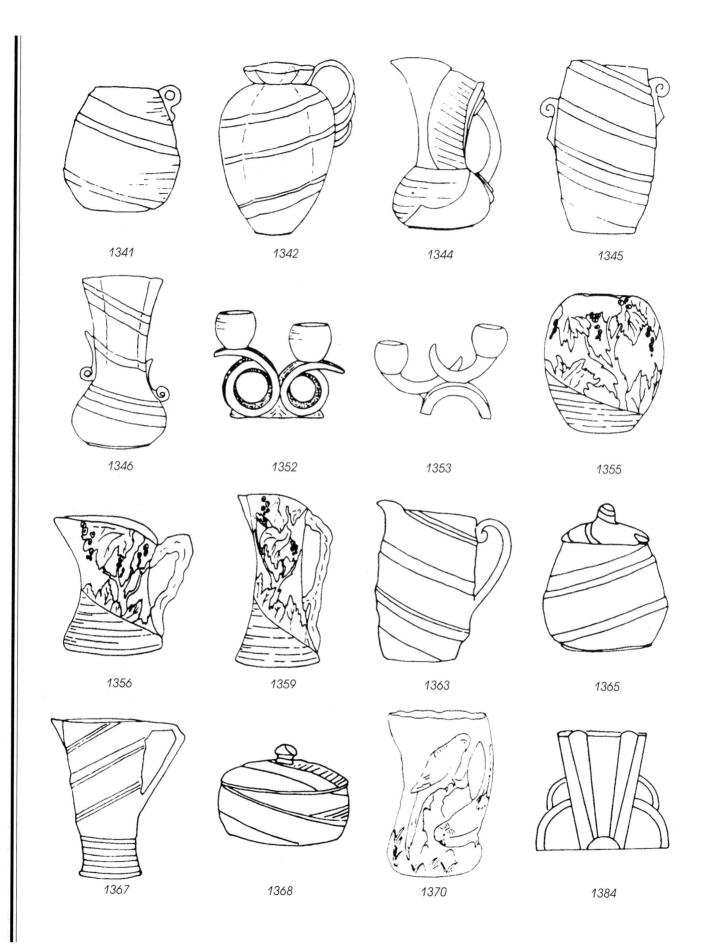

1341 1342 1344 1345

1346 1352 1353 1355

1356 1359 1363 1365

1367 1368 1370 1384

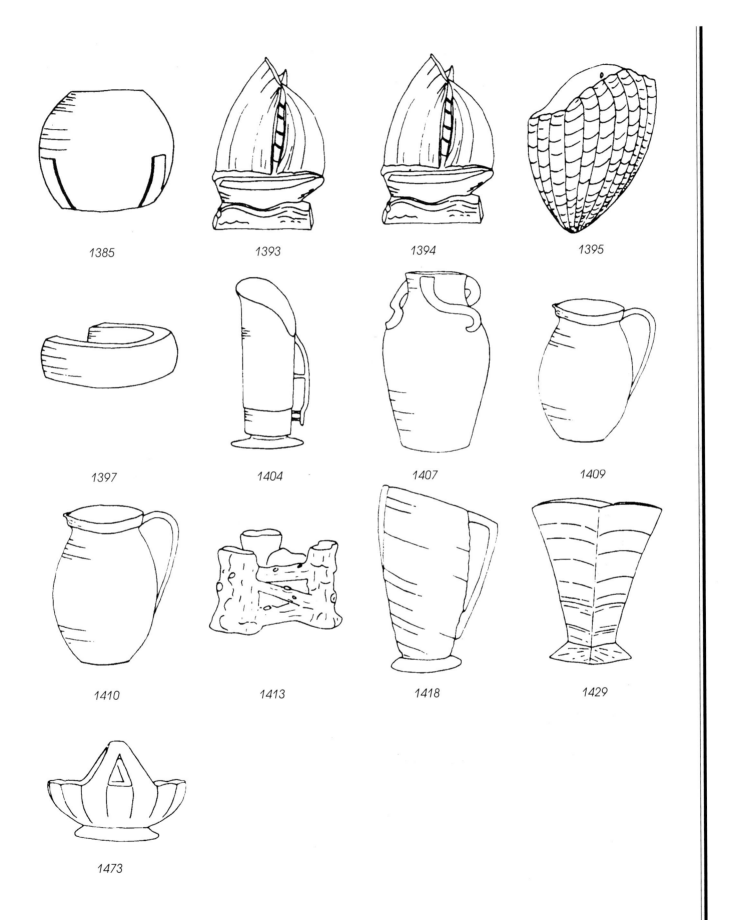

1385   1393   1394   1395

1397   1404   1407   1409

1410   1413   1418   1429

1473

Unnumbered Items

Napier Wash Set

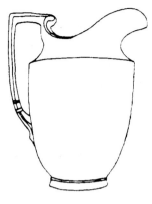

Jug 12$\frac{1}{2}$" h

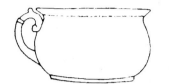

Chamber pot 4$\frac{1}{2}$" h   9" dia

Wash bowl 4$\frac{1}{2}$" h   16" dia

Soap dish 6" dia

Tooth brush holder 6" h

Silvo Wash Set

Jug 11" h

Chamber pot 5$\frac{1}{4}$" h   8$\frac{3}{4}$" dia

Wash bowl 4$\frac{1}{2}$" h   15" dia

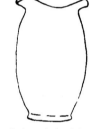

Tooth brush holder 6" h

Soap dish 6" dia

Silvo Dressing Table Set

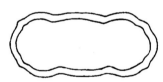

Tray No. 594   13$\frac{1}{2}$" l   6" w

Pot 3$\frac{1}{2}$" h   / 3" h

Ring stand 2" h

Hair baller 2$\frac{3}{4}$" h

Napier Dressing Table Set

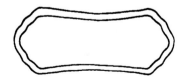

Tray 18" l   7"w

Pin-Stand 5$\frac{1}{2}$" h

Pin Tray 5$\frac{1}{2}$" l   3$\frac{1}{2}$" w

Pot 6$\frac{1}{4}$" l   4$\frac{3}{4}$" h 5" l   3$\frac{1}{4}$" h 4" l   2$\frac{3}{4}$" h

Ring tree 2$\frac{1}{2}$" h

Hair baller 6" l   3$\frac{1}{4}$" h

Unnumbered Items

Octagonal/Hexagonal Dressing Table Set

Tray no. 523 13$\frac{1}{2}$" l 9$\frac{1}{2}$"w   Hair baller   Pot 3$\frac{1}{2}$" h 3" dia   Pot 3$\frac{3}{4}$" h   Pin Stand   Ring Stand

3$\frac{3}{4}$"h 3"$\frac{1}{2}$ dia

Candlesticks

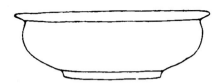

7" high   7" high   Wash bowl 15" dia 5" high

Jugs

7" h, 8" h, 10" h   6$\frac{3}{4}$"h, 7$\frac{1}{4}$"h, 8$\frac{1}{4}$"h   7" h, 8" h   4$\frac{1}{2}$" h

Size 3. 7" h   Three Sizes

Size 1. 8$\frac{1}{2}$"h

Unnumbered Items

Miscellaneous

Tea plate

Portland Vase 11" h, 8$\frac{1}{2}$"h

Roman 13$\frac{1}{2}$" h

10$\frac{3}{4}$"h

7$\frac{1}{2}$" h

7$\frac{1}{2}$" h

7$\frac{1}{2}$" h

7$\frac{1}{2}$"h 9" dia

6" h

6$\frac{3}{4}$"l 3$\frac{1}{4}$" h

Bread Plate 10$\frac{1}{4}$" dia

Cheese Dish 8"l 5"h

Chapter 9

MOULD NUMBER LIST & DATES

Dates

It is not always possible to give the exact dates of the mould design. However I have given dates based on the impressed marks and design influences. The registered numbers throughout the list give an exact date to the design providing much needed reference points. See registered number list page 81

Note on glazes and finishes.

No mention of the glazes has been made in this chapter since any item could have any of the six finishes. More detailed explanations and dates of glazes and finishes are given in the chapter 3 on decoration page 23.

Factory opened 1894.

Up to the outbreak of the First World War the shapes produced by S&C were essentially late Victorian in style. Many had recognisable classical shapes but often succumbed to the over-zealous use of Victorian embellishments.

Dates

It is not possible to state categorically when S&C started numbering their moulds. Where dates are given they represent the approximate year the moulds were first introduced.
By following popular trends and influences in design, coupled with the registered design numbers, the following dates have been arrived at. For more detailed explanations refer to chapter 4 on dating and chapter 2 on backstamps and factory marks.

Abbreviations:

- h..Height, 1..Length, dia..Diameter, w..Width, Reg No..Registered number, N/I..No information, *..Further information required. PL..Plate Number. Ribbed..A term used by S&C to denote little ridges around pots. This had the effect of making the item look hand turned.

Circa 1906

Mould No.	Description		Plate No.
1-74	N/I		
75.	Vase	9"h	PL10
76-126	N/I		
127.	Plant pot	7"h 9"dia	PL47
128-184	N/I		
185.	Jardiniere	5"h 4³/₄"dia	PL49
186-229	N/I		
230.	Clock	11¹/₂"h 9"w	PL36
231-254	N/I		

Circa 1913

Mould No.	Description		Plate No.
255.	Vase	13³/₄"h	PL15
256-261	N/I		
262.	Plant pot	6¹/₂"h 6³/₄"dia	PL48,49
263-272	N/I		
273.	Vase	9¹/₄"h	
274-278	N/I		
279.	Vase	11³/₄"h	PL6B
	Reg No 628381 19th Nov 1913		
280.	N/I		

Circa 1914

Mould No.	Description		Plate No.
281.	Vase	11¹/₂"h	PL8
	similar to 273		
282-292	N/I		
293.	Vase	11¹/₂"h	
	reg design no 634174 March 1914		
294-301	N/I		

August 1914-November 1918.

Although a small production was kept up during the war years no new designs were made. After the war production was restarted with most factories concentrating on re-establishing their old production. It was not until the 1920's that new designs were introduced.

302.	Jardiniere	8"h 10"dia	PL47
303-314	N/I		
315.	Plant pot	6"h 5$\frac{1}{4}$"dia	PL49
316-320	N/I		
321.	Vase	9$\frac{1}{2}$"h	PL18
322-334	N/I		
335.	Vase	10"h	
336.	Vase similar to 335	7$\frac{1}{2}$"h	
337.	Vase	12"h	
338.	Vase	13$\frac{1}{4}$"h	PL15
339-340	N/I		
341.	Jardiniere	6$\frac{1}{2}$"h 6"dia	
342-346	N/I		
347.	Vase	9$\frac{1}{2}$"h	PL18
348-349	N/I		
350.	Jardiniere on four feet scalloped top	5"h	
351-353	N/I		
354.	'Holborn' Re-issued	16"h	PL3
355.	Vase similar to 359	6$\frac{1}{2}$"h	
356.	N/I		
357.	Jardiniere	4$\frac{1}{2}$"h 4$\frac{1}{2}$"dia	PL12
358.	N/I		
359.	Vase	9$\frac{3}{4}$"h	PL18
360-361	N/I		
362.	Small plant pot	4$\frac{1}{2}$"h 4$\frac{1}{4}$"dia	PL49
363.	N/I		
364.	Vase	9$\frac{1}{2}$"h	
365.	Vase	11$\frac{3}{4}$"h	PL15
366-370	N/I		

Circa 1921

It is at about this time that Art Nouveau influences began to appear. Reference No 371 and 374. At the same time shapes were getting simpler both for production reasons and fashion, with the styles moving towards Art Deco, eg 417 and 419.

371.	Vase	9$\frac{1}{2}$"h	PL14
372.	N/I		
373.	N/I		
374.	Vase	12"h	PL16
375.	Tall vase	11$\frac{3}{4}$"h	PL11
376.	Vase Oval centre to match 375	7"h 11$\frac{3}{4}$"w	PL11
377-378	N/I		
379.	Vase		
380.	Oval vase similar to 376	5"h 8"w	
381-386	N/I		
387.	Vase	11$\frac{1}{2}$"h	PL8
388-398	N/I		
399.	Jardiniere embossed shells/scrolls similar to 401	4$\frac{1}{2}$"h 4$\frac{1}{2}$"d	
400	N/I		
401	Jardiniere embossed shells/scrolls similar to399	6$\frac{1}{4}$"h 6$\frac{1}{4}$dia	
402-410	N/I		
411.	Jardiniere	6$\frac{1}{4}$"dia 5$\frac{1}{4}$" h	
412-414	N/I		
415.	Vase *		
416.	Vase similar to 418	10"h	PL12
417.	N/I		
418.	Vase similar to 416	7$\frac{1}{2}$"h	
419.	Vase similar to 425 & 445	11$\frac{3}{4}$"h	PL7,17
420.	Vase	11$\frac{1}{2}$"h	PL9
421.	Vase	7$\frac{1}{2}$"h	
422.	Vase	8$\frac{1}{2}$"h	PL7
423.	N/I		
424.	Vase similar to 540		
425.	Vase similar to 419 & 445	9$\frac{1}{2}$"h	
426.	Vase	8$\frac{1}{4}$"h	
427-431	N/I		
432.	Vase	7$\frac{1}{2}$"h	PL19

Moulds Numbered 433, decorated in the embossed 'Wild Duck' design are of a later date. The original moulds were reused to expand the range. c. 1932/3. PL43

433.	Clock	5"h	PL34
	to go with vase 433		
433.	Vase	4"h	PL19
	to go with clock 433		
434-435	N/I		
436.	Bowl	$9^1/_2$"dia $2^1/_2$"h	PL71
	melon shaped, in the 1930's this came with bird etc		
437.	N/I		
438.	N/I		
439.	Vase	$7^1/_2$"h	
440.	Centre piece.	7"h $6^1/_2$"dia	PL45
441-444	N/I		
445.	Vase	$8^1/_2$"h	PL10,13
446.	Vase	$8^1/_2$"h	PL7
	similar to 421		
447-448	N/I		
449.	Vase	14"h	PL9
450-481	N/I		
482.	Clock	12"h	PL38
483.	N/I		
484.	Shaving mug	$4^1/_4$"h	PL29
485-488	N/I		
489.	Hexagonal bowl	$7^3/_4$"dia $3^1/_2$"h	PL82
490.	N/I		
491.	N/I		
492.	Rose bowl	$5^3/_4$"h $4^1/_2$"w	PL45
493-494	N/I		
495.	Vase similar to 510	$11^1/_2$"h	

Demand oscillated between the older more embellished styles of Art Nouveau and the newer simpler look. 496 is a good example. The origins of this mould come from the tulip, in a stylised form.

496.	Vase	11"h	PL8
497-508	N/I		
509.	Vase	10"h	
	similar to 496		
510.	Vase	$9^1/_2$"h	PL10
	similar to 495		
511.	Vase	$11^1/_2$"h	PL16, 33
	often found with clock 520		

Circa 1925

512-519	N/I		
520.	Clock	14"h $10^1/_2$"w	PL33
521.	Vase	12"h	
522.	Plinth round	$5^3/_4$"h $7^1/_4$"dia	
523.	Dressing table tray	$13^1/_2$"l	
	octagonal		
524-537	N/I		
538.	Vase	$7^3/_4$"h	
	similar to 539, 540, 541, 558, 562		
539.	Vase	$8^1/_2$"h	PL16
	similar to 538, 540, 541, 558, 562		
540.	Vase	8"h	
	similar to 538, 539, 541, 558, 562		
541.	Vase	$11^1/_2$"h	
	similar to 538, 539, 540, 558, 562		
542-547	N/I		
548.	Vase	$11^1/_4$"h	PL13
549-557	N/I		
558.	Vase		
	similar to 538, 539, 540, 562		
559.	Rose bowl	$6^1/_2$"dia $4^1/_2$"h	PL45
	not embossed.		

Mould No 559 decorated in the embossed 'Wild Duck' design is of a later date. The original mould was reused to expand the range in about 1932.

559.	Rose bowl	'$6^1/_2$" dia $4^1/_2$"h	
	embossed 'Wild Duck'		
560.	Jug	$8^1/_2$"h	PL52
561.	N/I		
562.	Vase	14"h	PL6D,14
	similar to 538, 539, 540, 541, 558		
563.	Jug	$6^3/_4$"h and $7^3/_4$"h	PL51
564.	N/I		
565.	Vase	$11^1/_2$"h	PL6A
566.	N/I		
567.	Vase	$11^1/_2$"h	
568-569	N/I		
570.	Vase	$8^1/_4$"h	
571.	N/I		
572.	N/I		
573.	Jugs	$7^3/_4$"h,$6^3/_4$"h,6"h,N/I,$5^1/_4$"h	PL53
	sizes 1-5.		

574.	N/I		
575.	Rose bowl with handles	8½"h	PL45
576.	Vase	11"h	
577.	N/I		
578.	Vase	6¾"h	
579-581	N/I		
580.	Plant pot on four feet	4"h	
582.	Vase similar to 583	11½"h	PL9
583.	Vase similar to 582	13¾"h	
584.	N/I		
585.	Vase *		
586.	N/I		
587.	Vase	9½"h	PL14
588-593	N/I		
594.	Sylvo tray	13½"l 6"w	PL21,23
595-599	N/I		
600.	Vase similar to 610,611	9½"h	PL18
601.	N/I		
602.	Jardinier similar to 603	5"h 6dia	

The plant pot 603 shows the gradual disappearance of the heavier embellishments in favour of pastoral or more natural looking impressions, (such as clouds leaves etc) which became popular in the 1920's.

603.	Plant pot similar to 602	6"h 7"dia	PL47
604.	Clock	12"h	PL38
605.	Heart shape clock to go with 606	9¾"h	PL32,44
606.	Heart shape vase to go with 605	7½"h	PL32
607.	N/I		
608.	Heart shape clock circular or square centres	11¾"h	PL31
609.	Heart shape vase to go with 608	9¾"h	PL31
610.	Vase similar to 600, 611	8½"h	PL19,36
611.	Vase	11¾"h	
612.	N/I		
613.	Vase	8"h	

614.	Vase	9¾"h	
615-621	N/I		
622.	Vase	14"h	
623-625	N/I		
626.	Vase similar to 627	7¾"h	PL34
627.	Vase similar to 626	10"h	PL6C
628.	N/I		
629.	Vase	11½"h	PL8
630-633	N/I		
634.	Vase for spills	6"h	PL19
635.	Vase for spills seen with silver rim *		
636.	Vase large spill vase similar to 634	8"h	PL19
637.	Vase	12"h	
638-639	N/I		
640.	Tray		
641-642	N/I		
643.	Cheese dish	7½"l	PL54
644.	N/I		
645.	Clock	11½"h	
646-647	N/I		
648.	Gothic style clock to go with vase	11½"h	PL30
648.	Gothic style vase to go with clock	10½"h	PL30
649.	Clock not embossed to go with vase 650	10"h	PL35

The mould numbers 649, 650 with embossed 'Wild Duck' design are of a later date than the plain ones of the same number. The original mould was simply reused to expand the range at a later date.

649.	Clock embossed 'Wild Duck' to go with vase 650	10"h	PL41
650.	Vase to go with clock 649	7½"h	PL35
650.	Vase embossed 'Wild Duck' to go with clock 649	7½"h	PL41
651.	Clock to go with vase 652	8¾"h x 11¼"w	PL39

652.	Vase *to clock 651*	$8^1/_2$"h	
653.	N/I		
654.	Sandwich tray *+ plates not numbered.*	$12^1/_2$"1 $6^3/_4$"w	PL46
655-658	N/I		
659.	'Scello' ware vase	$9^1/_2$"h	PL44
660-662	N/I		
663.	Embossed *Chinese ladies scene similar to 703*	12"h	PL57
664-665	N/I		
666.	Octagonal jug $6^3/_4$"h $7^1/_2$"h $8^3/_4$"h *at least 3 sizes.*		PL53,55
667-674	N/I		
675.	Wall plate	$11^3/_4$"1 8"w	PL46
676-677	N/I		
678.	Vase *similar to 679*	10"h	
679.	Vase *similar to 678*	11"h	PL17
680-688	N/I		
689.	Plant pot embossed, *Lord and Lady in Garden*	$4^1/_2$"h	
690.	Plant pot embossed, *Lord and Lady in Garden*	$5^1/_2$"h	
691-692	N/I		
693.	Plant pot embossed, *Lord and Lady in Garden, large*		
694-695	N/I		
696.	3pce clock set 'Lord and Lady' Clock $9^3/_4$"h x $7^3/_4$"w at base, vase $8^1/_2$"h x 4"w		PL42
697-699	N/I		
700.	Kingfisher bird *to go in bowl often No 436.*	$6^1/_2$"h	PL71
701-702	N/I		

There has always been a strong influence from China and Japan in English porcelain and vases 678 and 703 identify the particular popularity of the time. The launching of the smash hit musical Choo Chin Chow as well as the popular play *Lady Precious Stream* captured the public's imagination for all things oriental.

703.	Vase embossed *Chinese ladies scene similar to 663*	10"h	PL57

704.	Pot embossed *'Lord and Lady' scene*	$4^3/_4$"h	
705-710	N/I		
711.	Bowl embossed *marigold*	$11^1/_4$"dia, 3"h	
712-721	N/I		

Circa 1931

722.	Bowl embossed *octagonal fairy scene*	11"dia	

Themes such as fairies were made popular through James Barry's Peter Pan, seen here on 722 an Eastern shape.
NB. Further information on embossed ware will be found in the chapter on decoration page 157 – 158

723-725	N/I		
726.	Bowl embossed *garden scene*	$9^1/_2$"dia $2^1/_2$"h	PL71
727.	N/I		
728.	Rose bowl embossed *'Lord and Lady'*	6"h	
729-732	N/I		
733.	Pelican *with top hat & rock vase*	8"h	PL70
734-742	N/I		
743.	Airedale Terrier *(with vase 827 attached)*	7"h 9"1	PL70
744.	Clock	$10^1/_2$"h $10^1/_2$"w	PL37
745-751	N/I		
752.	Pekingese	$6^1/_2$"h $7^1/_2$"1	PL70
753-756	N/I		
757	Plant holder* *'Wild Duck' Reg No 762858*	large	
758-765	N/I		
766.	Camel *with saddlebags*	$5^1/_2$"h	
767.	Camel *with saddlebags on plinth*	$5^1/_2$"1 $4^1/_4$"h	
768.	Standing elephant	4"h	
769.	Standing elephant	6"h	
770.	Standing elephant	$7^1/_4$"h	
771.	Standing elephant	$8^1/_2$"h	
772.	Camel *standing with howdah*	9"1 x 7"h	
773.	Elephant *with howdah*	$8^1/_2$"h	

774.	Vase	12"h	
775.	N/I		
776.	Vase	6"h	
	fan shape embossed basket weave, and roses		
777-779	N/I		
780.	Vase	5"h	
781.	N/I		
782.	Vase		
	embossed 'Lord and Lady' in garden *		
783.	Clock.	10"h 14$\frac{1}{2}$"w	PL37
	The number is not clear*		
784.	Vase	7$\frac{3}{4}$"h	PL56
	embossed 'Wild Duck'		
785.	Vase	5$\frac{1}{4}$"h	PL56
	embossed 'Wild Duck'		
786.	Bowl embossed	9"sq	PL71
	'Wild Duck' square		
787.	Flying duck flower stand	7$\frac{1}{2}$"h	PL71
	similar to 700		
788.	Elephant	6"h	PL74
	with howdah		
789.	Elephant	7"h	
	with howdah		
790.	Vase	5$\frac{3}{4}$"h 8$\frac{1}{4}$"w	
	'Wild Duck' fan shape Reg No. 768168		
791-793	N/I		
794.	Swan		
795.	Swan		
796-797	N/I		
798.	Elephant		
	with howdah		
799.	Vase	9"h	
	'Wild Duck' Reg No 768695		
800.	N/I		
801.	Vase embossed	10"h	
	'Wild Duck' Reg No 768695		
802.	N/I		
803.	Candlestick	4"h	
	embossed 'Wild Duck' Reg No 769028		
804.	Box embossed	3"h	PL56
	'Wild Duck' Reg No 769029		
805.	Box embossed 2$\frac{1}{2}$"h 6$\frac{1}{2}$"1x4"W		
	'Wild Duck' (Reg No as 804)		

Circa 1932

806-808	N/I		
809.	Oval vase	9$\frac{1}{2}$"1 5$\frac{1}{2}$"h	
	embossed 'Wild Duck' Reg No 769285		
810.	N/I		
812.	Plant pot embossed 7"dia 6"h		
	'Wild Duck' Reg No 762858		
813.	Toby jug '	8$\frac{1}{4}$"h	
	Sam Weller' similar to 1231		
814.	Elephant	4$\frac{1}{4}$"1 4"h	
	with howdah		
815.	Elephant	4$\frac{1}{2}$"h	PL74
816.	N/I		
817.	Lion		
818.	Lion	6"1 4"h	
819.	Lion	12"1 6$\frac{3}{4}$"h	
	large as on 822		
820.	N/I		
821.	N/I		
822.	Lion	11"1 7$\frac{3}{4}$"h	PL72
	on plinth		
823.	Lion	9$\frac{1}{2}$"1 5$\frac{1}{2}$"h	PL72
	on plinth with tree stump vase		
824.	N/I		
825.	Lion	11"1 7$\frac{3}{4}$"h	
	on plinth with vase		
826.	Elephant	4$\frac{1}{2}$"h	
	with howdah		
827.	Vase	4$\frac{1}{4}$"h	
	with Airedale dog attached		
828.	Vase		
	ribbed Greek urn shape two handles		
829.	Jug	7$\frac{3}{4}$"h	PL78
	'Egyptian' Reg No 774557		
830.	N/I		
831.	Bowl		
	rectangular shape 'Egyptian' – Reg No 774557		
832.	Vase	7$\frac{1}{4}$"h	PL40
	'Egyptian' to go with clock 862 Reg No 774557		
833.	Vase	8$\frac{3}{4}$"h	
	'Egyptian' Reg No 774557		
834.	N/I		
835.	Jardiniere		
	'Egyptian' Reg No 774557		
836.	N/I		

837.	Rose bowl	6"dia 4$^1/_2$"h	
	'Egyptian' Reg No 774557		
838.	Vase	7"h	
	'Egyptian' Reg No 774557		
839.	Vase	7$^1/_2$"h	
	'Egyptian' Reg No 774557		
840.	Portland Vase	8$^1/_4$"h	
	'Egyptian' Reg No 774557		
841.	Vase	8"h	
	similar to 838 but with stand		
842.	Goblin	5$^3/_4$"h	
	with long tongue and five toes		
843.	Laughing cat	8$^1/_2$"h	PL73
	with bow tie		
844.	Laughing cat	8$^1/_2$"h	
	similar to 843 but with basket and detachable head		
845.	Goblin/Leprechaun	7$^1/_4$"h	PL73
	with vase similar to 842		
846.	N/I		
847.	Figurine vase	10"h	PL64
	Covent Garden flower girl		
848.	Vase	10$^1/_2$"l x 5$^3/_4$"h	PL58
	Oval 'Harvest Poppy'		
849.	Cheese dish	5$^1/_4$"l	
	decorated "From Southsea"		
850-857	N/I		
858.	Tree trunk rose bowl	5"h	
	embossed with flowers		
859-860	N/I		
861.	Vase	7$^3/_4$"h	
862.	Clock 'Egyptian'	9"h 7"w	PL40
	to go with 832 Reg No 774557		
863-864	N/I		
865.	Figurine vase	10"h	PL64
	Covent Garden flower seller		
866-880	N/I		
881.	Figurine of Spanish Lady	9$^1/_2$"h	PL63
882.	Vase *		
883.	Vase *		
884.	Vase *		
885.	N/I		
886.	Jug size 1	8"h	
887.	Lady figurine	5"h	
	in large flowing dress curtsying		
888.	Lady figurine	6$^1/_2$"h	PL65
	in feathered hat and muff		
889.	Lady figurine	7$^1/_4$"h	PL65
	in layered skirt shawl and bonnet		

890.	Lady figurine		PL65
	in hooped skirt and bunch of flowers		
891.	Dutch clog		
892.	N/I		
893.	Jardiniere	6$^3/_4$"h 4$^1/_4$"dia	PL47
894-897	N/I		
898.	Vase	10"l 5$^1/_2$"h	
	diamond shape Deco sun ray style		
899-901	N/I		

Circa 1934

902.	Vase ginger jar	7$^3/_4$"h	PL82
	shape similar to 903		
903.	Pot	7$^3/_4$"h	
	similar to 902, with lid embossed 'Harvest Poppy'		
904.	N/I		
905.	Vase	8$^3/_4$"h	PL58
	'Harvest Poppy'		
906.	N/I		
907.	Vase *		
908-916	N/I		
917.	Plant pot embossed approx 7"h		
	'Carnations'		
918.	N/I		
919.	Lady figurine	8$^1/_2$"h	PL63
	with ruffled sleeves holding skirt		
920.	Lady figurine	8$^1/_2$"h	PL63
	holding out skirts		
921-925	N/I		
926.	Plant pot	4$^3/_4$"h 4$^3/_4$"w	
	'Egyptian' Reg No 774557		
927-930	N/I		
931.	Figurine Pierrot	8$^3/_4$"h	PL63
932-934	N/I		
935.	Jug *		
936-943	N/I		
944.	Beaker/Vase embossed	6"h	
	'Arabian' scene		
945.	Pot with lid	5$^1/_4$"h 5$^1/_2$"dia	
	embossed 'Arabian' scene		
946-953	N/I		
954.	Jug *		
955.	Bowl *		

956.	Jug *		
957.	N/I		
958.	Rose bowl	6"h	PL45
	embossed 'Corn Flower'		
959-960	N/I		
961.	Shoe	5"1	
962.	Gnome	5"h	PL69
963.	N/I		
964.	Jug	7$\frac{1}{2}$"h	
	embossed 'Carnations'		
965	N/I		
966	Vase	6" h	
	embossed 'Carnations'		
967.	Vase	8$\frac{1}{2}$"	PL59
	embossed 'Cornflower'		
968.	N/I		
969.	N/I		
970-973	N/I		
974.	Vase oval		PL59
	embossed 'Carnations'		
975.	Vase *		
976.	N/I		
977.	Vase		PL59
	'Carnations'		
978-984	N/I		
981.	Beaver	6$\frac{3}{4}$"h	
	sitting up		
985.	Plant pot		
986.			
	N/I		
987.	Vase	11"h	
	embossed 'Cornflower'		
988-989	N/I		
990.	Bunny	5"h	
991.	Lion	7$\frac{1}{4}$"1 3$\frac{3}{4}$"h	PL72
992.	Puss in shoe	5"1 4"h	
993-999	N/I		
1000.	Mug ribbed		
1001.	Jug ribbed	7"h	PL60
1002.	Vase	11"h	
1003.	N/I		
1004.	Owl and tree	6$\frac{1}{2}$"h	PL75
	trunk vase		
1005-1006	N/I		
1007.	Vase small	5"h	

1008.	Vase	8"h	PL60
1009-1010	N/I		
1011.	Vase	8$\frac{1}{4}$"h	
1012-1013	N/I		
1014.	Vase	8$\frac{1}{2}$"h	
	bulbous base		
1015-1020	N/I		
1021.	Pixie	2$\frac{1}{2}$"h	
	sitting under mushroom		
1022.	Figure	5"h	
	of blackboy with banjo		
1023.	N/I		
1024.	Gnome	4$\frac{1}{2}$"h	PL69
	hugging his knees		
1025.	N/I		
1026.	Bunny	6$\frac{3}{4}$"h	
1027.	Bunny	8$\frac{1}{4}$"h	
1028.	Bunny	9$\frac{3}{4}$"h	
1029-1032	N/I		
1033.	Indian Chief	7$\frac{1}{4}$"h	PL66
	on rock		
1034-1037	N/I		
1038.	Bulldog	2$\frac{1}{2}$"h	
	sitting		
1039.	Kingfisher vase	6"h	PL71
1040-1042	N/I		

Circa 1935

1043.	Dog		
1044.	Bulldog	8$\frac{1}{2}$"h	
	with bow		
1045.	N/I		
1046.	Cat	6"h	
	standing frightened similar to 1313		
1047-1060	N/I		
1061.	Vase *		
1062-1063	N/I		
1064.	Bunny	4$\frac{1}{4}$"h	
	with posy holder/striker		
1065.	Bunny	6"h	
1066.	Rabbit		
1067.	Bunny	4"h	
1068-1069	N/I		
1070.	Flower jug	10$\frac{1}{2}$"h	PL77
	ribbed similar to 1071		

1071.	Flower jug *ribbed similar to 1070*	7"h	
1072-1074	N/I		
1075.	Vase *embossed flowers similar to 1077*	$6^1/_2$"h	PL61
1076.	N/I		
1077.	Vase *embossed flowers similar to 1075*	$8^3/_4$"h	PL61
1078	Jug *embossed flowers*	7"h	PL61
1079-1080	N/I		
1081.	Figurine *'Red Ridinghood' with picnic basket*	5"h	PL67
1082-1085	N/I		
1086.	Cat sitting	5"h	
1087.	Cat sitting	7"h	
1088.	Cat sitting	9"h	
1089.	N/I		
1090.	Mug *to match 1091*	$3^1/_2$"h	
1091.	Cider jug *ribbed design*		
1092.	Gnome *standing holding his sides*	$8^1/_4$"h	
1093.	Gnome *standing as 1092*	$9^1/_2$"h	PL69
1094.	Gnome *standing as 1092 & 1093 but solid at feet*	14"h	
1095.	Gnome *with pot*	$8^1/_4$"h	
1096.	N/I		
1097.	Gnome *with pot*	$9^1/_2$"h	
1098.	N/I		
1099.	Cat and basket		
1100-1108	N/I		

At this time a tremendous variety of styles were being designed. The 1109 classic Deco vase, the 1111 plant pot with Bacchus "God of Wine" theme, jugs 1114 and 1115 showing rural and animal influences, 1116 jug with the oriental dragon on the handle.

1109	Vase *deco style sun ray similar to 1384 wall vase*	7"h	
1110.	N/I		

1111.	Plant pot *on three feet 'Bacchanti' range*		
1112.	Vase *		
1113.	Oval vase *'Bacchanti'(embossed classical figures)*	$10^1/_2$"w $5^3/_4$"h	
1114.	Jug *embossed hollyhocks branch handle*	$7^3/_4$"h	PL78
1115.	Flower jug *acorn with squirrel handle*	$8^1/_2$"h	
1116.	Flower *jug with dragon handle*	$8^3/_4$"h	PL79
1117.	Dog *sitting large head*	7"h	
1118.	Dog *sitting 'Monty the mongrel'*	$6^1/_2$"h	
1119.	Dog *sitting with bow*	4"h	
1120.	Dog *sitting*	$3^3/_4$"h	
1121.	Dog *Terrier standing*	$4^3/_4$"h, $6^1/_2$"l	
1122.	Dog *Sealyham standing*	$3^3/_4$"h, $5^1/_2$"l	
1123.	Dog *Standing*	$3^1/_2$"h	
1124.	N/I		
1125.	Flower jug *'Bacchanti' range*	7"h	PL78
1126.	N/I		
1127.	Posy holder *Swan*	$5^1/_2$"l	
1128-1131	N/I		
1132.	Money box *Pig*	4"l	
1133.	N/I		
1134.	Jug *Cauldron*	$2^1/_2$"h	
1135.	Pot *Cauldron*	$3^3/_4$"h	
1136.	Bowl		
1137.	N/I		
1138.	Flower jug *with stork handle*	10"h	PL62
1139.	Flower jug *diamond shape*	$8^1/_2$"h	
1140.	Bowl *to go with 1134*	$2^1/_2$"h	
1141.	N/I		
1142.	Squirrel	$5^1/_4$"h	

No.	Description	Size	Plate
1143.	Squirrel	$6^3/_4$"h	
1144.	Squirrel	$7^3/_4$"h	
1145.	Squirrel	$8^1/_2$"h	
1146.	Squirrel	$9^3/_4$"h	
1147.	Jug *art deco style*	6"h	
1148.	Deco vase	$7^1/_2$"h	PL82
1149.	Vase	$7^3/_4$"h	
1150.	Flower jug *round ribbed*	$5^1/_4$"h	
1151-1152	N/I		
1153.	Small elephant *vase/holder*	3"h	PL74
1154.	Boy whistling		
1155-1156	N/I		
1157.	Mrs Duck *in fancy dress*	8"h	
1158.	Mr Duck *to match 1157*	9"h	
1159.	Cat *'Corkscrew Tail' similar to 1164,1163, 1162 Reg No806569*	$6^1/_4$"h	
1160.	N/I		
1161.	Girl Shy		
1162.	Cat *'Corkscrew Tail' similar to 1159,1163, 1164 Reg No 806569*	$3^3/_4$"h	
1163.	Cat *'Corkscrew Tail' similar to 1159,1162, 1164*	$7^1/_4$"h	
1164.	Cat *'Corkscrew Tail' similar to 1159,1162, 1163,*	8"l by 11"h	
1165.	N/I		
1166.	Vase	20"h	
1167.	Jug *with stag handle*	$8^1/_2$"h	PL79
1168.	Dish *oval*	$11^1/_2$" x $7^1/_2$" x 2"h	
1169.	"Lucky Pixie" *Large*	$5^3/_4$"h	
1170.	Girl *with banjo to match 1022*	5"h	
1171-1172	N/I		
1173.	Vase *ribbed*	7"h	PL76
1174.	Vase *for flowers triangular*	10"h	
1174.	Vase *There appear to be 2 vases with this number (not similar)**		

No.	Description	Size	Plate
1175.	Deco *vase Pilgrim shape*	6"h	
1176.	Vase *ribbed as 1177 & 1201*	$7^1/_2$"h	
1177.	Vase *ribbed*	$8^3/_4$"h	
1178.	Flower pot *ribbed*	$7^3/_4$"dia	
1179-1180	N/I		
1181.	Ashtray *with hare & striker No 1270*	$2^1/_2$"h	
1182.	Rabbit	$2^1/_2$"h	
1183.	Cruet set *ribbed*	5"dia $2^1/_2$"h	
1184.	Honey pot *ribbed*		
1185.	N/I		
1186.	Posy bowl	8"dia	
1187.	Spill vase	$4^1/_4$"h	
1188.	N/I		
1189.	Flower jug *triangular shape*	$11^1/_2$"h	

Circa 1936

No.	Description	Size	Plate
1190.	Flower jug *monkey nut Reg No 809067*	$7^1/_4$"h	PL79
1191.	Dog *sitting 'Joey' on collar*	5"h	
1192.	Dog *sitting 'Joey' on collar*	6"h	
1193.	Dog *sitting 'Joey' on collar*	8"h	
1194.	Dog *sitting 'Joey' on collar*	$9^1/_2$"h	
1195.	Flower jug *acorn with squirrel handle*	$7^1/_2$"h	
1196.	Flower jug *mushroom with two gnomes Reg No 809115*	$8^1/_2$"h	PL62
1197.	N/I		
1198.	Dish and stand *Oval watercress*	$11^1/_4$l 7"w	PL77
1199.	N/I		
1200.	Rabbit		
1201.	Vase	5"h	
1202.	N/I		
1203.	Alsatian dog sitting	9"h	
1204.	N/I		

No.	Item	Description	Size	Plate
1205.	Scotty dog	sitting Reg No 778504 Nov 1932	5"h	
1206.	Scotty dog	sitting Reg No 778504 Nov 1932	$6^1/_4$"h	
1207.	Scotty dog	sitting Reg No 778504 Nov 1932	$7^3/_4$"h	
1208.	Scotty dog	sitting Reg No 778504 Nov 1932	9"h	
1209.	Scotty dog	sitting Reg No 778504 Nov 1932	11"h	
1210.	Jar vase		$7^1/_2$"h	
1211.	Bowl		$1^3/_4$"h	
1212.	Candle holder ribbed		4"h	
1213.	Covered butter dish			
1214.	Flower pot ribbed		7"dia	
1215.	Flower pot ribbed		$8^3/_4$"dia	
1216.	Biscuit barrel ribbed		7"h	
1217-1220	N/I			
1221.	Gnome	with wheelbarrow	8"h	
1222-1225	N/I			
1226.	Wall plaque	Clown	9"h 6"w	PL80
1227.	Dog	standing	5"h	
1228-1229	N/I			
1230.	Toby jug	'Sarah Gamp'		PL68
1231.	Toby jug	'Sam Weller'	$6^1/_2$"h	PL68
1232-1234	N/I			
1235.	Posy	diamond shape	10"1 2"h	
1236-1237	N/I			
1238.	Elephant	standing on one leg in football gear	8"h	
1239-1243	N/I			
1244.	Dog	tall with collar		
1245.	Dog	Scottie	$5^3/_4$"h	
1246.	Dog	'Sammy' Reg No 813261 1936	$4^1/_2$"h	
1247.	Dog	'Sammy' Reg No 813261 1936	$5^1/_2$"h	
1248.	Posy ring		8"dia	
1249.	Posy bowl		6"dia	
1250.	Posy holder	Round	6"dia	
1251.	Posy	diamond shape	7"1	
1252.	Flower jug		6"h	
1253.	Flower jug		$6^1/_4$"h	
1254.	Flower jug		6"h	
1255.	Rabbit	mat holder and mats		
1256.	N/I			
1257.	Round vase		$7^3/_4$"h	
1258.	N/I			
1259.	Dog	Scotty	$2^3/_4$"h	
1260.	N/I			
1261.	Dog	Scotty standing	$7^3/_4$"h	
1262.	Dog	Scotty standing	8"h	
1263-1264	N/I			
1265.	Hare		3"h	
1266.	Ash Tray			
1267.	Flower pot	round ribbed	8"dia	
1268.	Flower pot	round ribbed	9"dia	
1269.	Flower pot	round ribbed	10"dia	
1270.	Hare	match holder	3"h	
1271.	Vase	for spills	5"h	
1272.	Deco style vase	shell design	$7^1/_4$"h	PL77
1273.	Flower jug	rope range		
1274.	Flower jug	hollyhock	$8^1/_2$"h	
1275.	Deco vase	shell design	6"h	PL77
1276.	Deco flower jug	shell design	6"h	
1277.	Deco flower jug	shell design as 1276	7"h	
1278.	Fruit bowl	shell design	11"dia	
1279.	Flower trough	shell design	$12^1/_2$"1	
1280.	Deco vase	shell design	$8^1/_2$"h	

1281.	Deco flower jug *shell design as 1276*	$9\frac{3}{4}$"h	
1282.	Flower pot *shell design*	$8\frac{1}{2}$"dia	
1283.	Flower pot *shell design*	$9\frac{1}{2}$"dia	
1284.	Lamb	4"h	
1285.	Lamb *as 1284*	5"h	
1286.	Cat *long neck*	4"h	
1287.	Cat		

Circa 1937

1288.	Miniature character jug *candle holder*	$3\frac{1}{2}$"h	
1289.	Miniature character jug	$2\frac{3}{4}$"h	PL81
1290.	Penguin	4"h	
1291.	N/I		
1292.	Chick *ash tray/bowl*	$4\frac{1}{4}$"h	
1293.	Duck *ash tray*	$3\frac{1}{2}$"h	
1294.	Rabbit *ash tray/bowl*	$5\frac{1}{2}$"l	
1295.	Dog *Griffon, sitting*	5"h	
1296.	Kittens *in a basket*	4"h	
1297.	N/I		
1298.	'Harry' the hare *Reg No 815840 1936*	$5\frac{3}{4}$"h	
1299.	'Harry' the hare *Reg No 815840 1936*	$7\frac{3}{4}$"h	
1300.	'Harry' the hare *Reg No 815840 1936*	$9\frac{1}{2}$"h	
1301.	Jug *		
1302.	Lop-eared rabbit *Reg No 815839 1936*	$5\frac{1}{2}$"h	
1303.	Lop-eared rabbit *Reg No 815839 1936*	7"h	
1304.	Lop-eared rabbit *Reg No 815839 1936*	$8\frac{1}{2}$"h	
1305.	Flower jug *bird and nest*	8"h	PL79
1306.	Vase *'Rope Range'*		
1307.	Deco vase *'Rope Range'*	$8\frac{1}{2}$"h	PL81

1308.	Vase *'Rope Range'*		
1309.	Vase *'Rope Range'*		
1310.	Jug *'Rope Range'*		
1311.	Book-end *various bunnies etc*		
1312.	Round posy *with 3 rabbits round edge*	$8\frac{1}{4}$"dia	
1313.	Cat *as 1046 scared*		
1314.	Posy trough	$1\frac{1}{2}$"h, $4\frac{1}{2}$"l	
1315.	Posy	6"l	
1316.	Posy	8"l	
1317.	Posy	12"l	
1318.	Flower jug *bunnies on handle*	$8\frac{3}{4}$"h	PL79
1319.	N/I		
1320.	Shoe ashtray	2"h	
1321.	Vase *commemorative George VI 1937*		
1322.	Toast rack	$6\frac{1}{2}$"l	
1323.	N/I		
1324.	Posy trough *angled*	11"l	
1325.	Posy trough *diamond shape*		
1326.	Posy holder *with figure*	$3\frac{1}{2}$"h	PL76
1327.	Deco style vase *with figure on one end*	$8\frac{3}{4}$"l	PL76
1328.	Woodpecker	4"h	
1329.	N/I		
1330.	Kingfisher	4"h	
1331.	Bird	$6\frac{1}{4}$"h	
1332.	Caricature *Dachshund*	$5\frac{1}{4}$"h 5"l	
1333.	Cat *Crouching*	4"h	
1334.	Foal *Standing*	4"h	
1335.	N/I		
1336.	Posy holder *with figure*	$7\frac{1}{4}$"h	
1337.	Posy holder *with flower seller*	$6\frac{1}{4}$"h	PL81

1338-1339	N/I		
1339.	Yacht solid with no posy holder	8³/₄"h	
1340.	Yacht posy holder similar to 1393 & 1394	12¹/₂"h	PL81
1341.	Vase Deco style	5¹/₄"h	PL83
1342.	Jug	6³/₄"h	
1343.	N/I		
1344.	Jug	9"h	
1345.	Vase Deco style	9"h	PL83
1346.	Vase	10¹/₂"h	
1347.	Vase		
1348.	Deco jug	12¹/₂"h	
1349.	Seagull Reg No 823083	3"h	
1350.	Seagull Reg No 823083	4"h	
1351.	Seagull Reg No 823083	5"h	
1352.	Posy holder Reg No 823084	6"h	PL81
1353.	Posy holder Reg No 823082	6"h	PL76
1354.	N/I		
1355.	Vase 'Autumn' range	7"h	
1356.	Jug 'Autumn' range	6"h	
1357.	Seagull similar to 1351,1350,1349,	2¹/₄"h	
1358.	Pot *		
1359.	Jug 'Autumn' range similar to 1356	12"h	
1360.	Flying duck similar to 1402,1401,1403	12"1	
1361.	N/I		
1362.	Sugar shaker deco style	5"h	
1363.	Jug Deco style	7¹/₄"h	PL78
1364.	Mug to go with 1363	3¹/₄"h	
1365.	Jam pot Deco style	4¹/₄"h	
1366.	Ashtray with various animals	5³/₄"1	
1367.	Jug	6"h	

1368.	Covered bowl 4¹/₄"dia 3¹/₄"h to match 1362 deco style		
1369.	Dog sitting puppy	5"h	
1370.	Budgerigar jar	7¹/₂"h	PL79
1371.	Rabbit	3¹/₂"h	
1372.	Polar bear	2³/₄"h	
1373.	Lamb standing	4"1	
1374.	Donkey	4"1	
1375.	Bird duck	3¹/₂"h	PL76
1376.	Bird	3"h	
1377.	Bird pigeon	4"h	

Circa 1938

1378.	Dog Terrier sitting	5"h	
1379.	Dog Terrier sitting	8"h	
1380.	Dog Terrier sitting	11"h	
1381.	N/I		
1382.	Dog Spaniel sitting	8"h	
1383.	N/I		
1384.	Wall pocket deco sun ray style similar to 1109	7¹/₄"h	PL80
1385.	Wall pocket Ribbed deco style similar to 1150		PL80
1386.	Rabbit	3¹/₄"h	
1387.	N/I		
1389.	Hare crouching	7¹/₂"h	
1390.	Koala bear on a log	4¹/₂"h	
1391.	Koala bear on a log	6"h	
1392.	Deco toast rack 2¹/₂"h x 6¹/₂"1		
1393.	Posy holder Yacht similar to 1340 Reg No 826482	5³/₄"h	
1394.	Posy holder Yacht similar to 1340 Reg No 826482	8¹/₂"h	
1395.	Wall pocket ridged with raised flowers or without	6¹/₄"h	
1396.	N/I		

1397.	Horse shoe shape posy		
1398.	Dog		
1399.	Frog	$2^1/_2$"h	
1400.	Tinies,	$1^1/_2$"h	
	combined number for a selection of miniature animals including bunny, mouse, dog, cat, duck etc, some have their own numbers		
1401.	Wall plaque	$6^1/_2$"l	
	Duck similar to 1360,1402,1403		
1402.	Wall plaque	$9^1/_2$"l	PL81
	Duck as above		
1403.	Wall plaque	5"l	
	Duck as above		
1404.	Jug	$6^1/_2$"h	
1405-1406	N/I		
1407.	Vase	$8^1/_2$"h	
1408.	N/I		
1409.	Jug	$5^1/_4$"h	
1410.	Jug	8"h	
1411.	N/I		
1412.	Dog	9"h	
	Airedale Terrier		
1413.	Vase	$4^1/_2$"h	
	Triple tree trunk		
1414.	Dog	5"h	
	sitting		
1415.	Dog	5"h	
	standing		
1416.	Vase	5"h	
	Tree trunk with Koala Bear on log		
1417.	Jug		
1418.	Jug	$8^1/_4$"h	
1419.	N/I		
1420.	'Lucky Pixie'	3"h	PL76
	sitting under toadstool with squirrel		
1421.	'Lucky Pixie'	3"h	
	sitting on mound		
1422.	Horse	$4^3/_4$"h	
	sitting similar to 1447		
1423.	Bear	3"h	
	standing		
1424.	Fox	$2^1/_4$"h	
	crouching		
1425.	Hippo	3"h	
	standing		
1426.	Bear/Panda	$3^1/_4$"h	
	standing		

1427.	Lamb	$3^3/_4$"h
	looking at tail	
1428.	Donkey	$4^1/_4$"h
	standing	
1429.	Vase	9"h
	tall diamond shape	
1430.	N/I	
1431.	Calf	$3^1/_2$"h
	standing	
1432.	Cat	
	three modles	
1433.	Dog	$3^1/_2$"h
1434.	Cat	
	lying down	
1435.	Jug	
	for cider 'Barrel' range	
1436.	Mug	$3^1/_2$"h
	'Barrel' range to go with 1435	
1437.	Jam pot	
	'Barrel' range	
1438.	Butter dish	
	round 'Barrel' range	
1439.	Cruet	$4^1/_2$"dia $1^3/_4$"h
	4 piece 'Barrel' range	
1440.	Butter dish/sweet tray	4"
	'Barrel' range	
1441.	Cigarette 'Barrel'	
1442.	Match holder	
	'Barrel' range	
1443.	Sauce bottle holder	
	'Barrel' range	
1444.	N/I	
1445.	Sauce boat	$5^1/_4$"l
	'Barrel' range	
1446.	Biscuit jar	
	'Barrel' range	
1447.	Foal	4"h
	sitting	
1448.	Bowl	
1449.	N/I	
1450.	Dog	
1451.	Stag	$5^1/_4$"h
	standing	
1452.	Jug	6"h
	'Mr Pickwick'	
1453.	Jug	6"h
	'Mr Micawber'	
1454.	Ashtray	$5^1/_4$"l
	round with animal (various)	

1455.	Ashtray	$4^3/_4$"dia
	Pond shape with animal (various)	
1456.	Mug	$3^1/_2$"h
	'Barrel' range	
1457.	Holder	3"h
	two tree stumps with two bunnies	
1458.	Leopard	$9^1/_2$"h
	attending to foot	
1459.	Serviette ring	
	with hare	
1460.	N/I	
1461.	Dog	6"h
	'Sammy' spaniel	
1462.	Dog	11"h
	'Sammy' spaniel	
1463.	Jug	$6^1/_4$"h
	'Neville Chamberlain'	
1464.	Tortoise	$3^1/_4$"1 $2^1/_2$"h
	one piece	
1465.	N/I	
1466.	Lizard	7"1
	on branch	
1467.	Lizard	6"1
1468-1469	N/I	
1470.	Cruet	
	pepper and salt	
1471-1474	N/I	

PL76

Circa 1939

1475.	Dog	$7^3/_4$"h
	sitting with paw raised	
1476.	Dog	11"h
	sitting with paw raised	
1479.	Posy	
	Curved with various small figures one end	
1480.	Posy	$5^3/_4$"dia
	Round with gnome in centre	
1481.	Posy	$8^3/_4$"dia
	Round with gnome in centre	
1482.	Candlestick	
1483.	N/I	
1484.	Top Hat	4"h
	with kitten Reg No 833892	
1485.	Candlestick	4"h
1486.	Pig	
	sitting	
1487.	Posy	$6^1/_2$"1 $4^1/_2$"h

	log with Koala Bear	
1488.	Posy	
1489.	Vase	
1490.	Vase	
1491.	Vase	
1492.	Duck	$5^1/_2$"h
	Reg No 833893 (1939) similar to 1498,1499	
1493.	Kangaroo	
1494.	Squirrel	4"h
	eating from bowl	
1495.	Vase	
1496.	Basket	
1497.	Rabbit one ear forward	3"1
	Crouching	
1498.	Duck	$5^1/_2$"h
	Reg No 833893 similar to 1492,1499,	
1499.	Duck	$4^1/_4$"h
	Reg No 833893 similar to 1492,1498,	
1500.	Panda	8"1 $4^1/_2$"h

Chapter 10

DECORATION NUMBERS AND DATES WITH HISTORICAL NOTES

Circa 1894 onwards.

The early decorations were often done without putting their number on the base. The pattern was largely hand painted onto an aerographed or plain background and given a name, now lost. The 1904 advertisement is typical of the type of pattern to be found. See page 10.

The illustration shows "Hand painted flowers, richly gilt birds, gilt foliage and handles". The numbers below the vases were the pattern reference numbers. Each shape was given a name e.g. **Manchester, Holborn** etc. which had popular associations of the time. Roses too were popular, so much so that some of the vases have been given rose names such as **York, Empress, Alexandra.**

Abbreviations: EX .. Exclusive to Shaw and Copestake.

The following list may or may not be 'Daisy' marked

UNNUMBERED DECORATIONS

The following unnumbered decorations were used at various times from the founding of the factory up to the outbreak of the Second World War.

FLOWERS, 1894 onward. PL 12, 14, 16, 18, 46, 50.

Flower themes were used a great deal, influenced by the great botanical artists of the time and by English gardens which were world famous.

SWANS, C 1894 onward. PL16, 19, 49, 51.

The Swan pattern was a popular and well loved universal design and was used by many manufacturers. These royal birds on a pair of vases would be shown with two different pictures to make a pair.

RURAL SCENES, C 1900-1920's. PL 15, 19, 49, 50.

These became popular during the early part of this century.

With the expansion of the Industrial Revolution the countryside began to disappear, the designs were a reminder of what was passing into history. They tended to show scenes of all aspects of rural life in nostalgic and idealised form. They became a record of the 'good old days'. Some transfers are signed Harold E. Peace.

Ploughing PL33

FOLK TALES, C 1900-1920. PL18.

These were often depicted in some form or other; the shepherd and shepherdess is an example. Not shown.

HUNTING, C 1910 onward. PL49

A popular past time.

Numbered Decorations.

1330	Chequered Line in black. **PL29.**
1392	Windmill with clouds, trees, lake and boat **PL53.**

Circa 1920

	Silhouette of sailing boat in harbour. **PL53.**
1500	'Moonlight' no moon hut on island. (largely hand painted) EX Found on blue, pale blue, black, pink and plum colour backgrounds. **PL9, 10, 11, 26, 35, 37, 45, 46.**

A similar pattern in blue is made by another manufacturer but the trees are curved.

1682	Speckled purple glaze with daisy print top. **PL51.**
1760	Black with roses. **PL 19, 38, 45, 47.**

The discovery of Tutankhamun's tomb in 1921 and various archaeological finds provoked tremendous interest in all things to do with the desert.

1907	Egyptian style (small) EX **PL 17, 47.**
1926	Egyptian style
1949	Irises on blue **PL52.**

Circa 1925.

The improvements in transport encouraged the middle classes to travel widely particularly to Europe. Many places became popular subjects for use as decoration. Good strong colours were in favour of which **Venetian** and **Basket of Fruit** are good examples.

1977	Venetian EX **PL8.**
1978	Venetian EX similar to 1977.

Lovebirds provided a popular romantic theme in songs. This registered design show a definite eastern influence with lanterns and birds but the lady is wearing a 1920's style dress of Parisian haute couture fashion.

1993	Lovebirds variation. EX
1996	Basket of fruit. **PL13.**
2007	Lovebirds. EX. **PL7, 8.**
2029	Venetian, boat with oarsman, lantern, butterflies. EX.
2046.	Red roses with green leaves on black (2 side by side).

Lawrence of Arabia also popularised the desert with his exploits and book *The Seven Pillars of Wisdom*. The desert became a romantic theme taken up by films and artists alike. White slave trade.

2092	Camel and rider in desert, buildings in background **PL32.**
2096	Butterflies, trees and palace. **PL47**
2098	'Devon Days' coaching scene.
2099.	Figures in front of tower, fence & trees, village behind **PL34.**
2106	Chinese lanterns and butterflies. EX. The lanterns and butterflies are from different patterns but are unique to S&C.
2139	Irises with stems overlaid in gold, on pink. **PL48.**
2157	Moonlight, with moon, tower and island. EX. **PL25.**
2207	Man on camel with two palm trees.
2212	Arab on camel. **PL55.**
2216	Kneeling Japanese lady with round coloured lanterns or flowers behind. **PL38.**
2226	Arabic palace with palm tree, camel & rider.
2304	Kneeling Japanese lady with willow bridge in background.
2334	Portland vase. **PL5.**
2337	Pair of apples and foliage Lustreware. EX. **PL20.**
2355	Chinese scene bridge and figures like willow pattern.

2392	Windmill on lake with boat and trees.
2398	Background of desert tents, figures round fire in front.
2431	Two birds over a lily pond. **PL6A**
2436	Gondola on lake with tree and harbour steps, Hand painted. EX **PL39**.
2438.	Palm trees, desert palace and figure. **PL17**.
2480	Spray of flowers heads, rose, berries, leaves & bird. **PL19, 21.**
2481	Spray of flowers heads, rose, berries, leaves & bird. **PL19, 21.**
2495	Swans and cygnets on lily pond. **PL 6C, 30.**
249-	Windmill on hill landscape.
2541	Palm tree, houses and boat.
2548	Fishing; two boats, seven figures, palace behind. (Shrimping) **PL31.**
2603	Country inn with trees, 3 pitched roofs and people. EX.
2604	Arab scene in front of buildings, people, donkey, tree, etc. **PL 52.**
2642	Garden with path and steps, flowers, birds and tree.

In the 1930's nostalgic country themes became even more romanticized, with cottages and inns often featured.

2675	'Scenes of the Old Country' on blue. EX. **PL24, 55.**
2683	'Scenes of the Old Country' on red. EX.
2706	Hut on seashore with flowers, hand painted. EX.

LORD AND LADY, C 1929/30 (Cellulose). EX. **PL42.**
Various scenes of lady and gentleman in 18th century dress walking through an oriental garden.

SCELLO WARE, C 1928/29 TO 1935. **PL 39, 44.**
This was a word invented by S & C for their cellulose products other than the ones with specific names, before the name 'SylvaC' was adopted. See chapter 2 on factory marks.

WILD DUCK, 1931 (Cellulose). EX. **PL41, 43, 56.** Registered design see list.
This pattern effectively combines two major influences of the time, the natural rural look and the Chinese use of the duck, quite typical of the 1930's. Some pieces appear in matt glazes at a later date.

EGYPTIAN, 1932 (Cellulose). EX. **PL39, 78.** Registered design see list page...
This design is taken from a patchwork, showing a papyrus boat, swords, snake, master and slaves. This uses the fashionable influences of Egyptian discoveries. Some pieces appear in matt glaze at a later date.
Illustration of range page 64.

HARVEST POPPY, 1932/33 (Cellulose). EX. **PL44, 58.**
This was a popular subject particularly after the First World War. The flowers are stylized but accurate, a popular way of designing.

ARAB GATEWAY, C 1933/34 (Cellulose). EX.
This embossed scene looks like some of the ancient city gates in Morocco where espionage and rumours of the white slave trade were rife. Morocco was easily reached across the Mediterranean by yacht or steam ship. It was popular with English high society and the much married multi-millionairess Barbra Hutton. The publicity and gossip that surrounded these people and events added to the romanticism of foreign travel and the desert. Both were popular themes for artists.

CARNATION/CORNFLOWER, 1934 (Cellulose). EX. **PL59**.
Registered design see list and factory marks.
This design seems to have been called by two names.

All design Numbers after 2714 have the Combined SylvaC daisy mark.

This does not apply to cellulose in general.

2714	Garden path with flowers.
2744	Villa with garden on lake with boat.
2761	Arab scene of square, donkey, people and buildings.
2784	Boy and girl in Swiss costume with mountain behind. EX. **PL50**.
2795	House on a hill with path, trees and flowers (Cottage Garden) **PL47, 54**.

Circa 1934.

2830	Design unknown, mentioned in correspondence 1934.
2839	'Old English Inns'. EX.
2851	Windmill cottage and boat. EX.
2876	'Lady Jane' in sedan chair with man on horseback (18'th.Century dress).
2885	Lake, tree and flowers.
—	Dutch scene windmill on lake, two figures in traditional costume. Hand painted. **PL37**.
—	Windmill on a hill overlooking lake and hills. Hand painted. EX. PL44.
—	'Summertime' Garden and path flanked by hollyhocks.

Circa 1935

Matt Glazes (not daisy marked) in dark brown and deep blue were limited productions. Green, beige and others followed.

'Aurora' type glaze. Dark blue background with splattered and dribbled glaze. Predominantly white mixed with brown and pale blue applied to look like a star-burst C 1936/7
Reproduced in the 1960's in high gloss glaze.

Cellulose numbers in "SylvaC Ware" EX

0319	Mottled matt, various colours.
0323	Floral daisy, flowers in yellow and orange tints.

Backgrounds and other colourings in brown.

Circa 1937

0343	Green top blending down to a soft tone of yellow, pink rising from foot.
0344	Pinkish-brown top blending down to yellow and having a bluey-green foot.
0353	Crocus, colourings as above.
0354	Red floral, in shades of pink, background of mottled matt buff, finished in brown and gold.
0355	Floral border, colourings as for 0323.
0356	Floral, in shades of pink, background in mottled matt buff, finished in brown and gold.

SYLVAC DEALERS

Cottage Curios
Telephone 0843 602806
39 High Street,
St Peters,
Broadstairs,
Kent.

Darrell Willis-Utting
Telephone 05394 88662
Bay House,
Fallbarrow Road,
Bowness-on-Windermere,
Cumbria LA23 3DJ

Olive M. Caple
Telephone 081 644 4896
Attends Antique Fairs in the South East.

Reg Penney
Telephone 0272 658468
Attends Antique Fairs in the South and South West.

Lee and Rachel Emery
Telephone 0272 861806
Attends Antique Fairs mainly in the South.